Early
Broadstairs and St Peter's

IN OLD PHOTOGRAPHS

James Henry Summerson (Uncle Mack) 1876–1949, who brought joy and laughter to young and old.

Early
Broadstairs and St Peter's

IN OLD PHOTOGRAPHS

Collected by BARRIE WOOTTON

Alan Sutton

Alan Sutton Publishing Ltd
Phoenix Mill · Far Thrupp · Stroud · Gloucestershire

First Published 1992
Copyright © Barrie Wootton 1992

This book is dedicated to my father,
Arthur Ernest Wootton, who has lived
most of his life in the village of
St Peter's.

British Library Cataloguing in Publication Data

Wootton, Barrie
Early Broadstairs and St. Peter's in Old Photographs
I. Title
942.2357

ISBN 0–7509–0054–7

Typeset in Sabon 9/10.
Typesetting and Origination by
Alan Sutton Publishing Limited.
Printed in Great Britain by
The Bath Press, Avon.

Contents

Foreword

I have always had a deep affection for Broadstairs.

I was born in Ramsgate, not more than 100 yards from the Derby Arms which my grandmother ran, but my family soon moved to Broadstairs where we lived for a number of years.

A bungalow called Adstone in Linden Avenue was my home, and when it became time for my schooling I was sent to Stone House Preparatory School which was at the bottom of our garden. Later my education was furthered by my attending (along with Mr Ted Heath) Chatham House School.

Many memories come flooding back when Broadstairs is mentioned. Uncle Mack (whose Talent Contest I won) walking down the High Street, smoking his pipe on his way to the sands and another day's work.

And a beautiful lady photographer and her two pretty daughters whom I got to know slightly. One daughter was to become a household name in the 1940s: Dinah Sheridan, the lovely film star of *Genevieve* fame.

I also remember with affection the 'Playhouse Theatre' (which looked as if it had been built of plywood and corrugated iron), the 'Bohemia' and the little cinema at the end of the arcade in the High Street.

My days of innocence, playing on the sands and enjoying long walks in the surrounding countryside, led me to the North Foreland to peer through large gates at the incredibly prolific writer of the Billy Bunter stories, Frank Richards, pottering in his garden wearing a smoking cap and cycle clips.

All this fresh air and exercise was good for the appetite and I used to go to Marchesi's to buy a meat pie. To pay for such luxuries I earned a few bob by selling programmes for the town's Water Gala.

In my childhood, the Grand Hotel was the centre of evening entertainment. Evening dress was a must and the chef's wife, Mrs Pears, who was an opera singer, could be seen and heard.

Gwen Lewis and her concert party appeared at the Garden on the Sands and, every Thursday night, Uncle Mack gave a 'White Night', appearing without the black greasepaint.

I hope that this short reminiscence will, like the book, bring back happy memories of Broadstairs and its surrounding villages.

Frank Muir

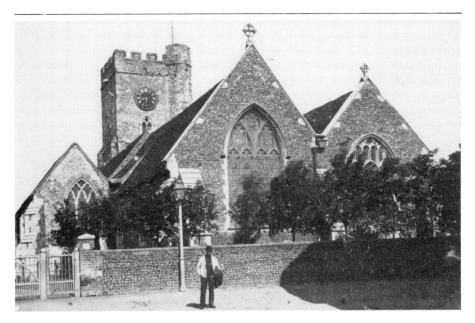

Introduction

St Peter's Church was in existence in 1070 as a chapel of ease to St Mary's Church of Minster. It was the governing centre over the hamlet of Bradstowe (now Broadstairs) once situated within its parish. Years of expansion have seen their roles reversed.

Parish rule by St Peter's churchwardens and Justices of the Peace ended when Broadstairs itself became a parish in 1856. Holy Trinity Church, built in 1829/30, became the spiritual and governing centre of Broadstairs. In later years parish rule for both village and town passed to the local Health Board, instigated on 7 July 1879, which in turn was superseded by the Broadstairs and St Peter's Urban District Council on 10 January 1895. This body has been incorporated into the Thanet Council since 1974.

In the early nineteenth century both town and village were rural backwaters: St Peter's a farming community and Broadstairs a small fishing community. Before Holy Trinity Church was built there had been a shrine to our Lady of Bradstowe in Broadstairs. Pilgrims came here to pray and seek a cure for their ailments. The shrine was so revered that passing ships would lower their sails in deference. By the 1870s, however, the only pilgrims were visitors seeking the sea air, sun and salt water as a rest or cure for their ailments. In 1824, the young Princess Victoria, later Queen Victoria, stayed at Pierremont Hall with her mother, the Duchess of Kent.

Broadstairs developed a more genteel and sedate nature compared to her larger sister towns of Ramsgate and Margate, to which the populace of London found easier access by either road or paddle-steamers. Later, in 1862, the arrival of the railway in Broadstairs was further to alter the town's circumstances.

The Broadstairs hermit, John Edward Roberts.

Charles Dickens found the hamlet of Broadstairs by accident while on a walk from Ramsgate in 1836. In 1837 he returned for the first of many visits. The great author loved the small town and his gift for words allowed him to paint in print the people and buildings of the watering place. He drew inspiration from many hours spent in its public houses, soaking up the atmosphere and nature of its inhabitants, and, in the peace and quiet, wrote some of the most memorable chapters of his novels of the social life of our nation. In later years Dickens found the town too noisy and commercialized and, in 1851, he took his last leave of Broadstairs.

Dickens left a legacy in print; we have a legacy in old buildings to pass on to future generations: St Peter's Church, Ranelagh Assembly Rooms, Reading Street's Flemish-gabled houses, the York Gate, the Royal Albion Hotel, the pier and Bleak House to name but a few. This town and village are rich in old buildings and famous people: Thomas Crampton, the famous engineer born in Broadstairs, Lord Northcliffe, owner/editor of the *Daily Mail*, Daniel Mason, shoe-polish millionaire, all have graced the town or district with their presence.

The last man I will mention is Sir Edward Heath. Broadstairs born and bred, he is best remembered as the Prime Minister who led this country into Europe.

The evolution of transport has seen the shrinking of distances between towns and villages. The meadows and cornfields that once surrounded our village and town have given way to tarmac, bricks and mortar. In the following pages I invite you to see some of those views and people of yesteryear that our grandfathers knew so well.

Barrie Wootton

Westwood, Northwood and St Peter's

Aerial view of St Peter's and surrounding fields, early 1930s. In the bottom half of the photograph is the Ramsgate/Margate Road, Poorhole Lane and the Westwood Road. On the left of Poorhole Lane is Westwood Lodge, built and owned for many years by the Herepath family. To the left, behind the houses along the Westwood Road, can be seen the brickfields belonging to Paramors. These brickfields were among the many dotted around St Peter's at the turn of the century. The top half of the photograph shows St Peter's village and church with the gasworks and power station to the left, followed by the Shallows leading to Dane Valley.

No. 3 Paramor Cottages, Westwood Road, St Peter's, *c.* 1910. Postcard of the house and its neighbours showing clearly the length of front garden which was lost when the Westwood Road was widened.

Entitled 'Cross Roads', this view, looking towards St Peter's, is of the junction of Bromstone, Fairfield and Pysons Roads. The trees and fence on the opposite corner to the signpost mark the boundary of Bromstone House grounds. When I was a boy, there was a pond near the clump of trees. The photograph was taken in 1900.

Bromstone Road, St Peter's, further along from the Cross Roads. Bromstone Road is now much wider, with small housing estates on both sides. Both pictures depict horse-drawn vehicles as this was the only means of travel in the rural countryside surrounding St Peter's at that time.

The old windmill at Northwood, c. 1901. Mentioned in a small booklet called *Field-Rambles*, this windmill is one of four that could then be seen in and around Broadstairs and St Peter's.

Northwood Wesleyan chapel in Northwood Road, next to Tabernacle Cottages, *c.* 1920. Once the sister to the Wesleyan chapel in Ranelagh Grove, St Peter's, it is now a private house.

The entrance to Dane Court on the St Peter's to Margate Road, looking towards Margate. The entrance on the right is still there. I remember some of the trees on the left but even these have gone now. Among the many owners of Dane Court in its final years was Mr A.T. Batchelor who also owned Bleak House at the same time. Mr Batchelor converted Dane Court into twelve flats but from 1954 these remained unoccupied until the house was demolished in 1960.

Vicarage Street, St Peter's, showing the narrow Vicarage Hill, *c.* 1930. To the right, half-way up the hill, is the entrance to Oaklands Court. Note the profusion of foliage, sadly lacking today. In the 1861 Census, Vicarage Street was called St Peter's Street; by the next Census it had reverted to its former name.

Front view of St Peter's Old Vicarage, 1917. Built in 1726, this Georgian vicarage was situated where the bungalows of Canterbury Close are built today. The architect of the house was a Mr Grey, who was also the architect of Holland House at Kingsgate. *Mocketts Journal* states that an earlier vicarage lay further to the west, but according to the resident vicar, Leonard Rowntree, it was in a state of decay in 1618. This statement establishes that a vicarage has been in the St Peter's environs for 350 years or more.

The garden at the rear of the vicarage. The first vicar to live in this fine house was the Revd J. Dean and the last was the Revd Thomas Estlin Prichard who later became Archdeacon of Maidstone. The vicarage was finally demolished in 1963 and another piece of St Peter's history was gone for ever.

Oaklands Court, *c.* 1913. This imposing building is situated half-way up Vicarage Hill on the right, going towards the church of St Peter. It was once the home of Henry Sheridan, relative of Thomas Sheridan, actor, writer and father of the Rt. Hon. Richard Brinsley Sheridan, the famous MP and dramatist. In later years, Oaklands was turned into a Preparatory School for Boys under the auspices of A.W.W. Gordon, after which C.R. Ellis and then E.W. Fiske ran the school until the early 1920s.

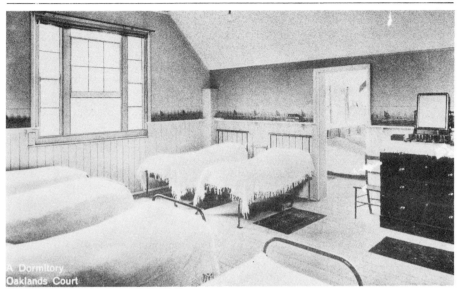

Interior of Oaklands: a dormitory of spartan cleanliness. (Note no floor covering – only slip mats and bare boards!)

Interior of Oaklands: a typical 1913 classroom, heated by an enormous fireplace, with old style school desks – the racks in front of each one were used to contain books.

The dining room at Oaklands. The school must have had considerable sporting prowess judging by the trophies displayed on the top table.

A shady walk in the grounds of Oaklands, surrounded by hedges and trees, sadly no longer seen in this locality. The earliest games of cricket were played on these school grounds as there were no public recreation areas available.

This fine building still remains within the grounds of Oaklands Court, now surrounded by bungalows and houses. This view can be seen from Oaklands Avenue and also shows some of the additions which have been made to the house in recent years.

The Wheatsheaf public house, 1920. The Wheatsheaf was the first public house you saw if you entered St Peter's from Margate. Owned by Cobb's, the Margate brewers, the Wheatsheaf is now a restaurant. In 1841 the landlord was Charles Silk. In 1879, another landlord of the Wheatsheaf was ordered to close his drinking-water well as it was deemed unhealthy and fresh water was available from the Broadstairs Water Company founded in 1859 by Thomas Crampton.

Vicarage Street, St Peter's, *c.* 1920, looking down Vicarage Hill. In the foreground on the left is Lockes the florist, followed by Calava Cottages and their gardens, pulled down to make way for the public toilets and King's wet-fish shop, later the Toc H. The high wall and trees beyond belong to Blagdon House, now an old people's home. On the right is the Salem Baptist church next to the Wheatsheaf. The tranquillity of this picture is a far cry from today's bedlam of traffic.

St Peter's village sign, *c.* 1926. This was the first site of the village sign. On the right, in the distance, can be seen first Vye's shop and then Hopeville farmhouse, built in 1682 for Richard and Sarah Mockett.

The village sign was brought about by a speech made by the Duke of York (later King George VI) at the Royal Academy in 1920 on the revival of village signs. The *Daily Mail* newspaper organized a competition and exhibition offering a total of £2,200 in prizes for the design of the best village sign. Ten awards were made and a design, from which this sign was constructed, won first prize of £1,000. The St Peter's sign was designed by a young Ramsgate resident, Mr P.H. Matthews, and was to have been erected in front of Nuckells Almshouses. However, because of delays in receiving a favourable answer from the Trustees of the Almshouses, on a suggestion from Councillor, the Revd Ridgeway, the sign was placed on the corner of the church wall where anyone entering the village could see it.

St Peter's Church, 1890. St Peter's and its sister churches of St Lawrence and St John form a trinity of churches, all chapels of ease to Minster Abbey, which in turn was overseen by Canterbury. St Peter's is first mentioned in 1124 by Abbot Hugo II and Archbishop William de Corbeuil of Canterbury.

St Peter's Church from the churchyard. In 1200 St Peter's became parochial, with the proviso that the priest and parishioners went to Minster, once a year in procession, to show they were subject to the abbey.

Taxi outside St Peter's Church gates, photographed in 1908 by a friend of Mr Shepperd the taxi owner. The walls and gates seen here were erected in 1875 and the gates were designed by Mr Seddon. The pillars originally had gas lamps on their tops and the stonework on which the boy is sitting has since been removed.

St Peter's Church, *c.* 1880s. An extensive restoration programme was embarked on in 1859–65 under various vicars, the first being the Revd Sanderson Robins. Part of the work carried out was the building of the wall and gates, seen here hung on two massive pillars surmounted by large gas lamps.

The east window of St Peter's Church, dedicated to the Glory of God and the memory of Mervyn Noott, 2nd Lt. of the Buffs, who was killed at Radinghem Wood in France on 20 October 1914. The window was designed by Mr Louis Davis and placed in the church in 1921.

The Revd Alfred Whitehead, vicar of St Peter's from 1871 to 1898, saw many changes to the church. In 1872 he undertook the restoration of the church roof which was completed within two months. He further undertook two more restorations, one to commemorate the Golden Jubilee of Queen Victoria and the other the Diamond Jubilee of 1897. A year after this came his death. A memorial plaque to this man can be found on the north arcade of the church. He was born in the town of Ramsgate.

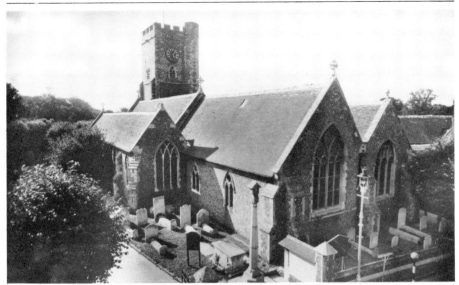

An unusual view of the church during the 1930s. The tombstones clustered round the church are the oldest in the churchyard, the earliest being that of William Norwood dated 20 May 1623.

Postcard showing the Revd C.H. Matthews, vicar of St Peter's *c.* 1920, seated on the left, with other members of the clergy who are unknown to me. During the First World War the Revd Matthews went with the RAF to Izel Lee Harnean (near Arras in France), leaving the Revd Harcourt Charles Vaux Snowden as priest in charge at St Peter's.

RED LION HOTEL, ST. PETER'S.
BROADSTAIRS.

Proprietor - - - - GUS HARRIS.

The Red Lion Hotel, St Peter's, Broadstairs. Note the three doors and the flag-pole which has since disappeared along with the two lamps over the doors.

St Peter's High Street, 1919. Ghostly figures on both sides of the road indicate where children have moved while Mr West of Whitstable was taking this photograph.

St Peter's High Street, *c*. 1880. One of the earliest postcards of my collection. On the left can be seen the Red Lion sign with a bunch of grapes hanging beside it (an old-fashioned sign for a public house). The Red Lion itself is out of sight, obscured by what was then St Peter's Post Office, run by Miss Harriet Busbridge, daughter of Isaac Busbridge of the same address who was a shoemaker. The Red Lion today replaces the previous single-storey, thatched Red Lion pulled down in 1876 after being used as a hospital for smallpox cases. The outbreak of the disease killed ten villagers.

Looking down St Peter's High Street, *c.* 1919. On the left hand side is Creasy's slaughterhouse, followed by their grocery store, the only grocery store in the village allowed to sell wines and spirits.

Village children pose for posterity, 1920s. On the right of the High Street is Clarks the shoemaker followed by King's wet-fish shop and, next door, Mr Horton the saddler; then comes Tippledore Alley, followed by the Crown and Thistle public house. The sign for W. Harlow is placed by a narrow opening which led to the Groom's Cottage which lay behind these since demolished buildings. Mr Harlow was a jobbing master or haulage man using horse-drawn vehicles.

High Street, St Peter's, *c.* 1927. On the right the nearest shop to the camera is Creasy's chocolate and confectionery shop, while opposite is the Crown and Thistle, and just seen walking across the pavement are the infants school children coming out of Tippledore Alley (earlier known as Ranelagh Passage).

The High Street in the early 1900s, showing on the right Mr Pointer's house and garden pulled down in 1910 to widen the road, and later the site of the Parish Hut. On the other side of the road, facing Pointer's, is an ironmongers, later to become Bishop's the watch repairers and now a block of flats.

Mr and Mrs Richardson, the Crown and Thistle's last landlord and his wife standing behind the public bar.

Darts room of the Crown and Thistle. Those regulars known to the author are, second from left: Bob Brenchley. Centre: Walter Goodhew. Third from right: Mr Richardson (the landlord). Second from right: Tom (surname unknown).

The High Street, 1908. On the left can be seen H. Shrimpton, the cycle maker and retailer of Pratt's motor spirit (petrol); above his shop is Piggott's coal office. Across the road is a clear view of the two cottages belonging to Pointer's the builder. Note the width of the road, 14 ft 6 inches. (Printed by permission of Kent County Library.)

The High Street, c. 1926. Orlebar House can be seen next to the Parish Hut which was erected in 1922 having originally been used as a cinema at Stonar Camp, Sandwich in the First World War. Note the magnificent wrought-iron gates to the school entrance.

Poor of KENNETS lived HERE (handwritten note)

Nuckells Almshouses, High Street, St Peter's – a print by W.P. Crawford. Built in 1805 at the expense of Mr Brown, they replaced a previous workhouse built in 1753. The cost was £1,405. Thomas Wall was installed as master of the workhouse to care for forty-five poor souls and was paid 4*s.* per head a week to feed and clothe each one; this sum was reduced to 3*s.* 6*d.* in May 1822.

yr poor lived here (handwritten note)

St Peter's High Street, 1920s. On the left in the foreground is Mr Percy Pettman's grocery store. Mr Pettman started his store in 1907 and passed the business to his daughter, Mildred, who continued to run it until 1960 when it became Dolmans Groceries. Next to Pettman's is Warren's, the butchers run by 'Chum' Warren and his sister until the 1970s. Then follows Shrimpton's Cycle Works. Pettman's store was originally built as a Wesleyan chapel.

The High Street viewed from the Coves. On the left is St Peter's Hand Laundry drying grounds then the road to Ranelagh Grove; opposite is Lloyds Bank. On the right is Farthings, the Post Office, preceded by Grove House, the home of St Peter's Hand Laundry.

The Coves, St Peter's. This very old house has part of its construction dating back to Queen Anne times. The gardens have, in the last decade, aroused interest due to the extensive chalk caves which served as air-raid shelters in both world wars. It was once the home of Miss Olive Raven who was sister to Dr Hugh Raven, the well-known Broadstairs family doctor.

US personnel searching the rubble following the crash, on Sunday, 27 April 1952, of an American Thunder-jet from Manston on to Lloyds Bank and the ironmongers shop which was on the corner of Ranelagh Grove and the High Street. The pilot, Captain Clifford Fogarty, and Mr and Mrs Read, owners of the ironmongers, were all killed in this tragic accident. (Printed by permission of Kent Fire Brigade.)

Owned by Mr Charles Newbolt, the enterprising publican of the Red Lion Inn, St Peter's, the Ranelagh Tea Gardens were built on land once belonging to the Mocketts. In the grounds were a bandstand and a platform 55 ft by 18 ft wide covered by a canopy for dancing (shown above). The Assembly Rooms and a steward's cottage, adorned on the gable with figures of Neptune and attendants, completed this establishment. In later years, when its popularity waned, the Assembly Rooms became St Peter's Boys' School and the steward's cottage the schoolmaster's house.

Ranelagh Grove, St Peter's, *c.* 1928. The houses to the left have been built since Ranelagh Tea Gardens ceased trading. In the distance can be seen the Assembly Rooms partially hidden by the small cottage in the centre of the picture. The wall and shrubs to the right once surrounded the dancing platform, replaced in 1871 by a Wesleyan chapel. The young girl to the left is believed to be Miss Violet West.

Green Lane, St Peter's, late 1920s. On the left, the tall trees and privets surround the grounds belonging to The Lodge, a large house whose grounds were later developed into Salts Drive and the small group of bungalows. The other houses, to the right, looked out over open fields.

Green Lane, St Peter's, *c.* 1930, looking towards St Peter's Road from the direction of Broadstairs. Just how narrow Green Lane was can be seen by the width of the road shown in the foreground. The signpost points to a narrow footpath which led to Upton and Dumpton by yet more narrow footpaths, some still in existence today.

St Peter's Road. The railings on the right surround what was then Claringbould House, a private residence with extensive grounds, later used as Selwyn House Preparatory School. On the left, the cottage depicted has been demolished together with the wall which continues along the road behind it. Of all the trees seen here only a few exist today, the rest having been chopped down to make way for housing development.

'Val Dora', St Peter's Road, *c.* 1905. Once the home of the Marchioness Menabrea di Val Dora, the house took its name from her surname. In later years it became known as Chedworth and was a training establishment for private nurses. After the Second World War, it became known as St Christopher's and was turned into three flats. It was demolished to make way for a small housing estate now known as St Christopher's Green.

Upton Road, from St Peter's Road looking towards Upton Farm. Upton Road was part of an ancient track which ran from Joss Bay through Callis Court, Bairds Hill, Sowell Street and on to Upton Farm. Once only a cart track, it was used extensively for the transference of seaweed and farming goods, as each of those places mentioned incorporated farms. Only in the late nineteenth century did some of this track become a hard road.

St Margaret's, St Peter's Road, *c.* 1907. This large house is now No. 27 St Peter's Road, and was for many years run as a boarding house by Misses Reardon and Ratcliffe. From 1906 to 1910 it was, as shown here, a girls' school run by Miss McLaren.

Christmas, 1905.

With Christmas Greetings and all happiness and Prosperity in the Coming Year from Mrs. Surtees.

"True and constant Friends be with you always."
—SHAKESPEARE.

Hilderstone,

St. Peter's, Thanet.

Christmas Greetings from Hilderstone House, 1905. Hilderstone has had a chequered career. Once the home of Mr L.A. Elyard, who had the house erected in 1883, it was obviously still a private house in 1905. Later the home was used as an annexe to Alexander House School and is now an Adult Learning Centre of some repute.

St Peter's Road, *c.* 1911, according to the postcard. However, the view is, in fact, of Gladstone Road, Broadstairs, as there are no two-storey houses of this design in St Peter's Road, they are all three-storey.

Mother Lived Here

Edge End Road, *c.* 1900, before any of the houses had been built on the right hand side of St Peter's Road between Edge End Road and Gladstone Road. The houses in the middle are now part of Hilderstone House Annexe and the path and green in the foreground are no longer visible because of housing development.

Circus elephant being admired by schoolchildren, *c.* 1905. Over the years there must have been many strange sights that Broadstairs people can recall, but none stranger than a string of Sangers Circus Elephants parading down the High Street for their daily dip in the sea! Here a baby elephant is surrounded by children on what is now Edge End playing fields but was then Sangers Circus Pitch.

Captain H.H. Balfour MC, MP. Today it is hard to visualize that seventy years ago there was no public highway between Edge End Road and Vicarage Hill and it was not until Thursday, 14 July 1929 that Captain H.H. Balfour, MP for Thanet, officially opened this main road into Broadstairs. Other local dignitaries seen here are Councillors Hemstead and Foster.

Motor cavalcade. After cutting the tape to open officially Broadstairs Road, a cavalcade of cars led by Mr and Mrs Balfour and Mr and Mrs Bing then travelled to the bottom of Vicarage Hill where a vote of thanks was given to Mr Balfour and his wife from Councillor Oak-Rhind. The cost of building the road was £15,412 of which £7,091 was a government grant from the Ministry of Transport.

A sketch of the proposed Catholic church at the junction of St Peter's Road and Broadstairs Road. This particular design was a far cry from the church which was eventually built.

Our Lady, Star of the Sea, Roman Catholic church, c. 1940. This church was consecrated in 1931 but was not fully completed until 1961. An unusual feature is its outer finish of flint which was used on much earlier buildings in Broadstairs and St Peter's, this being the only local building material available.

Broadstairs Police Station, 1904. Built in 1898, the station was under the jurisdiction of Kent County Constabulary and consisted of living-in accommodation for one Inspector and one Constable, three cells and various interview rooms. The first Inspector was W. Stanford, who took up his duties on 12 August 1898 and remained until April 1903. The station was enlarged at a later date and is now supervised by Ramsgate Police, there being no police presence after 5.30 p.m. in the evening!

No. 47 Gladstone Road, 1904. This building is now Haddon Dene, a private school. The untouched land behind shows how much development has occurred over the last eighty years.

Mildredsbourne School, 1906. No. 45 Gladstone Road was a private school for young ladies, seen here at hockey practice. The building in the background is Broadstairs Police Station belonging to the County Constabulary.

Haddon Dene School, Gladstone Road. A later view of No. 47 showing the houses built on either side. In the distance, the sails already removed, is the windmill at Pierremont just before its demolition in 1909.

The Broadway, Broadstairs. These imposing shops are all that was built in 1904/5, following a grandiose scheme to provide Broadstairs with a Town Hall, Opera House and roof garden restaurant plus shopping centre. Prior to 1900 there were only two big houses and their gardens on this site.

The tram route from the Broadway looking down to St Peter's Park Road in 1904 before any housing development occurred. On the right are the old library, fire station and Council Offices. The tram rails to the left are for the top road and those to the right are for the bottom road to the seafront.

St Peter's Park Road, 1913, showing the development of this road in comparison with the photograph on the previous page. The Social Security Offices now stand where John Perry's coal yard and the fire station are depicted on the right.

Our Lady, Star of the Sea. This shows the interior of the Roman Catholic tin church, once situated in St Peter's Park Road. Built in 1888, it was the second Roman Catholic church to be built in Broadstairs after the Reformation. The first was a small room in Gladstone Road. In 1931 the parishioners transferred to the new church in Broadstairs Road. Incidentally, my father and uncle were altar boys to this church in their younger days and would arise early to clean and dust the altar before Sunday services.

St Joseph's Convent, 1907. Built in 1906 this beautiful building was originally used as a school for young ladies, and run by the Sisters of Christian Retreat who came to Broadstairs from France in 1903. They first settled in a house called Roseneath once situated in St Peter's Park Road. The message on the back of this postcard is a Christmas greeting from one of the Sisters of the convent. The Sisters of Retreat were founded by the village priest of Le Fontenelles, whose primary aim was to educate children of the poor. I am grateful to Sister Eta for this information.

Bairds Hill, St Peter's, c. 1905, looking towards the junction with St Peter's Park Road. On both sides of the road are tall privets and iron railings belonging to large private houses and preparatory schools. At the bottom of the hill, to the left, was The Banks, a house owned by the Vye family, famous Kentish grocers. On the right, facing them, is The Hermitage, a Tudor house of great age reputed to be haunted. Both are hidden from view by the lush foliage.

Church Street, St Peter's, 1910, from Albion Road. To the right is Napier Road, named after Sir Charles Napier, famous statesman and soldier. The shop on the corner with the Hovis sign is Southee's the bakers, later to become Thomas Green's the chemist. On the opposite side is Dunford's, a general grocers store, later to become Walker's the well-known bakers.

St Peter's recreation ground, 1946. In 1946 Broadstairs and St Peter's celebrated with a Gala Fortnight. A gymkhana was held at St Peter's recreation ground on Thursday, 8 September, and among those present were Broadstairs Gala Girl, Miss Daphne Howard of Edge End Road, and her two attendants, Miss Jean Allen of Inverness Terrace and Miss Eileen Bircham of Palmers Green, here seen seated in the front row of the spectators.

St Peter's end of Beacon Road, 1938, on a wet winter's day, with the entrance to Westover Road on the left and Cecilia Grove on the right. The tall cast-iron pole on the corner of Cecilia Grove was used to take the overhead cables for the trams. The houses on the right of Beacon Road cover a meadow where my father used to take carpets for beating at 2s. 6d., as vacuum cleaners had yet to be developed commercially.

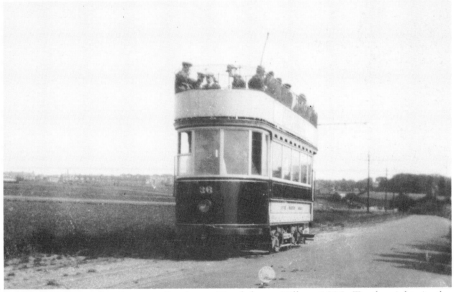

A No. 36 tram makes its way slowly up Northdown Hill, c. 1925. To the right, in the distance, is the St Peter's Tram Depot, while on the left are the open fields now covered by St Peter's council estate.

Church Street, St Peter's, in 1920. Looking towards Albion Road, the first building on the left is Noble's Workshop, followed by two pairs of houses now demolished. To the right by the gas lamp is Speak Road, named after the famous explorer. On either corner of this road were two shops: the off-licence to the left and, on the right, Albert Olive's shop which sold everything. 'Sooty' Olive gave my father his first job as a schoolboy which was errand boy and carpet beater. The nickname 'Sooty' came from the fact that Mr Albert Olive was also a chimney sweep.

Northdown Road looking towards Church Street. An oil painting of Northdown Road (called Granville Road in the 1861 Census). The road is little more than a cart track. The thatched buildings to the left are part of a farm which, together with the wall, obscures a duck pond which was situated on the corner of Northdown Road and Church Street. The trees on the right are part of what was then Mockett's Orchard. (Printed by permission of Noble's, the funeral directors of St Peter's.)

Northdown Road, 1917. On the left is the meadow where Harrison's dairy cows once grazed. Opposite the gas lamp is the entrance to Magdela Road on the corner of which was Eudens, the newsagents and tobacconists. The tall chimney in the distance belongs to the power station which first supplied power for the trams and then the houses of Broadstairs and Margate. The building to the right is the tram depot built in 1900.

Northdown Road, late 1940s. An almost identical view to the one above but thirty years later. The power station is now obscured by a row of semi-detached houses and the road has been widened. The chestnut fencing in the foreground surrounds a piece of wasteland later used to build St Peter's Ambulance Station and an auxiliary fire station. The first shop on the right is Mr Broadway's, the greengrocers.

Church Street, *c.* 1920, at the junction of Northdown Road and Victoria Road. The three cottages to the right have been demolished and replaced by a row of shops. The three ladies are standing outside No. 52 Church Street, home of Frank Austen who, in 1929, had the idea of relaying radio programmes to his neighbours by cable. His company was called Broadcast Relay Services Ltd, later to become Rediffusion. Of the three ladies, the one nearest to the camera is Mrs Bell Barwick and the baby in the pram is either Phyllis or Joan Hill.

Hopeville, Church Street, 1906. Built in 1723, this was the second home of the Mockett family. The well-known artist, Walker Sickert, resided here from 1934 until his death in 1942. The house has remained in the Mockett family since 1723 and the ground to the right of the house was once Mockett's Orchard.

Church Street at its narrowest point, 1914. With hardly any traffic this street is a far cry from today's bedlam. On the left is Hopeville Farm wall and Mockett's old farmhouse built in 1682. The taxi sign to the right is where Edward Shepherd kept St Peter's Garage Taxis. The house just visible behind the trees to the right is The Limes, once the home of Mr Wotton of Thompson & Wotton, the brewers.

A summer view of Church Street, 1922, with the entrance to Hopeville Farm on the left. Notice the steep drop at the gate. This was because Church Street had been gradually built up and the farm was many feet below the road level.

Hopeville Farm, 1900. A really rural scene showing the most well-known farm of St Peter's with the tower of the church depicted in the background. Taken over by the Mockett family in the early seventeenth century, the farm became known as Hopeville Farm in 1824. (I am indebted to Mr Fowles of High Street, St Peter's for this photograph.)

The junction of High Street and Church Street. The first building on the left in Church Street is Vye's, the grocery shop, once The Star Inn. The site is now occupied by the Memorial Hall. Ward's, the chemist, is situated next to Bayford's sweetshop where, as a young boy, my father could purchase tiger nuts, licorice wood and penny gob-stoppers while on his way to school.

Transport

No. 37 Tram in the depot yard at the bottom of Northdown Hill, 1924. To the left is the power station chimney and just visible to the right, behind the tram, are The Cabin Refreshment Rooms. Especially built to serve tea and buns to the trams' crews, the first owner was a man called Mr George Bass. (Printed by permission of Mr D.W.K. Jones.)

The brake majestic. Until the advent of the tram and motorbus, brakes, wagonettes and stagecoaches were the only means of public transport to the more remote parts of Thanet. This particular brake is headed for Pegwell Bay and is pictured outside Eveling's, the drapers shop in Broadstairs High Street opposite Queens Road.

Tram repair tower. Used to repair the overhead electrical cables conducting the trams, this tower weighed 30 cwt and was hauled up by means of ropes at the side. This is one of the most treasured photographs in my collection as the workmen depicted includes my grandfather. The photograph was taken at Bradshaw's Corner at the junction of Salisbury Avenue and Dumpton Drive. Left to right: Harry Durle, Thomas George Wootton, Charles Willis, the engineer. (Printed by permission of Mr D.W.K. Jones.)

The staff of the Isle of Thanet Tramway Company depicted outside the St Peter's depot situated at the bottom of Westover Road and Northdown Hill, 1901. This depot was built in 1900 to house firstly the trams and later East Kent Road Car Company buses, the trams' successors in 1937.

Snow clearing at Beacon Road, *c.* 1922. The front tram has a blade on the front to crudely scrape the snow from the tram lines. Eagle House can be seen in the background to the left with its stone eagle perched on the roof, while the snow plough passes the door of No. 15 Beacon Road. (Printed by permission of Mr D.W.K. Jones.)

Maintenance staff of St Peter's Tram Depot in 1923 showing the skilled workers who maintained the trams from 4 April 1901 until 24 March 1937. Back row, left to right: Daddy Miller, Jack Whitmore, Harry Gilham, Stan Parker, Bob Baker, Alf Greengrass, George Anstey, Jim Kemp, Bert Overall. Front row: Harry Goodban, Tom Buckingham, George Raynor, Jack Hammond, Charlie Fryer, Frank Holton. (My thanks to Mr Bob Prett for the loan of this photograph.)

Trams undergoing repair. This gives some idea of just how far maintenance and repair were carried out at the St Peter's depot and the skills that were involved in keeping these rattling giants on the rails. (Printed by permission of Mr D.W.K. Jones.)

Last day of the trams, 1937. On 24 March 1937 the last trams ran from Ramsgate to Margate changing mayors at the boundary of each town. The scene above was taken at St Peter's depot where the population turned out *en masse* to watch the last of these dinosaurs run into the depot. The following day, the East Kent Road Car Company buses took control of the roads.

The Star Inn, Ramsgate/Margate Road, *c.* 1930. An unknown outing to the old pub, obviously not to beat the boundaries but only to quench their thirsts! The charabancs were built by Thorncroft's and belonged to B. Redbourne and Sons of Granville Garage, Thanet Road, Ramsgate, who maintained a service between Ramsgate and Margate from June 1929 until October 1935 when the concern was taken over by East Kent Road Car Company.

An East Kent single-decker bus negotiating a steep hill in Broadstairs High Street, 1931. The East Kent Road Car Company Ltd was formed on 11 August 1916 from five local bus companies. Henceforth, until 24 March 1937 when the last trams ran, the competition for passengers was on. The above vehicle was a Tilling-Stephens B10/C/2 purchased in April 1930 and requisitioned by the MOD in 1940 and never heard of again. (Printed by permission of Saunders of Canterbury.)

Day Trippers' Express, 1923. The arrival of the railways in Broadstairs in 1862/3 signalled the end of Broadstairs as a quiet backwater; the town was now within reach of the metropolis. The above train of at least eight coaches is just about to enter Broadstairs station. To the left the cinder footpath can be seen alongside the track. Both locomotives belong to the South Eastern and Chatham Railway and were built at Ashford. (Printed by kind permission of Mr Clive Baker.)

Northdown, Reading Street and Kingsgate

North Foreland Tea House. These tea rooms are situated almost opposite the North Foreland lighthouse. The waitresses are in Dutch costume but it was only named the Dutch Tea House many years later. This establishment is now a hotel.

HIGHEST POINT IN
ISLE OF THANET (049)

The Thanet Needle (the Pepper Pot). Once situated at the top of Northdown Hill and called the 'Whitfield Tower', this monument owes its existence to the eccentric Lord Holland who, in 1763, built a rather shorter tower (up to the first mantle) to the memory of Robert Whitfield from whom he bought his Kingsgate Estate in 1760. In 1818 the Trinity House Brethren had the tower heightened to its present structure for use as a navigation aid, and so it remained until 20 March 1978 when it was blown down in a gale. Two hundred and fifteen years of history had gone forever. Incidentally, the highest point in Thanet is not Northdown but the Prospect at Minster.

Reaping at Northdown 56

'Reaping at Northdown'. The cornfield depicted is where Prince Charles Road and Coronation Close of St Peter's housing estate are today. In the distance, to the left, is the Red Beacon, while the houses are all that had been built on the right hand side of Beacon Road. The large house on the extreme right is Callis Court.

The last hours of the Red Beacon as workmen begin to demolish this well-known landmark which had stood since 1827. Built by Trinity House to assist shipping to navigate the dangerous Margate Sands, the beacon is believed to have been pulled down in 1934. (Printed by kind permission of Mr Graham Noble.)

Reading Street end of Beacon Road, which derives its name from the Red Beacon once situated behind the houses to the right, 1916. Two modes of transport are shown here: the horse and cart on the left, and a hand barrow on the right which belonged to S.A. Cuthbert and Co. of No. 146 Northdown Road, Margate. The man standing by the barrow is obviously delivering a brand new dustbin and has walked here and will walk back to Cliftonville – no wonder there were so many cobblers in the area!

Kimberley, Reading Street. Once tea rooms, this building, I am told, was intended as a public house but because of the nearness of the White Swan it became a private residence. It is now the surgery for Dr Jepps and stands at the crossroads of Reading Street and Convent Road.

Rimpton Court, Reading Street. This was a boys' private school run by Mr Hawtrey in the 1920s and '30s. Mr Hawtrey was the nephew of Charles Hawtrey, a well-known Victorian dramatic actor and no relation to the 'Carry On' film actor. In March 1948 the Home Office sanctioned a loan of £6,744 to purchase Rimpton as a children's home. This has since been closed and the house divided into private apartments.

The White Swan, Reading Street. An old inn, once owned by the Thompson and Wotton Brewery and frequently used by smugglers, dating back to the 1700s. Note the effigy of a swan perched on a pole by the pub's main door. In 1913 this public house was extensively rebuilt and today bears no resemblance to the above photograph taken in 1902. The one-time landlord, William Harlow, also hired out horses and traps which were in stables situated where the big tree stands on the left of this photograph. Mr Harlow's daughter recalls her father teaching North Foreland Lodge schoolgirls how to ride and being called out at all hours of the day to take people by trap to Broadstairs railway station.

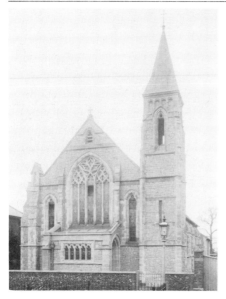

St Andrew's Church, Reading Street, 1911. Built on land once owned by Rimpton Court, the church was consecrated by the Archbishop of Canterbury on Monday, 10 April 1911 and cost £3,500 to build. An unusual added feature of the church is a mosaic of the Last Supper which came from the Tait Homes chapel which is mentioned in the following section.

The Bing family has been associated with Reading Street for over a hundred years. Back row, left to right: Isabel Clara Bing born 1899, Eva Mary Bing born 1897, Sidney Bing born 1899, wife Alice born 1897, Edward Stace Bing born 1901. Front row: Leonard Bing born 1902, Alfred John Bing born 1905, Ernest Leslie Bing born 1907.

Reading Street Panto, 1925, in Reading Street Hall. Entitled 'Red Riding Hood of Reading Street', this pantomime was enacted by the St Andrew's Dramatic Society and was written by the Revd H.N. Gibson who also played Seawolf, the smuggler.

Broadstairs and St Peter's Fire Brigade attending a fire at two cottages in Trinity Square, Reading Street. The fire broke out at 9.30 p.m. on 22 July 1909, the occupants being Mr Edward Fagg and Mr and Mrs Brookes and their four children. The fire was started by the younger child, Frank Brookes, who lent out of a window holding a lighted candle which set the curtains alight and, in turn, the thatched roof. Both families escaped without harm but their dwellings were destroyed. The cottages had formerly been a notorious public house called The North Star renowned for its smuggling connections.

Reading Street School, 1938. Back row, left to right: Peter Doyle, Arthur Ovenden, Bobby Nuttings, -?-, Donald Petman, Jimmy Lawrence, Wesley Britten, Jimmy Haddon, Ralph Smith, Ron Bushell, John Newing. Middle row: -?-, Sylvia Sutherland, Sheila Bing, Eileen Bird, Doreen Doyle, Reg Bushell, Godfrey Wake, Tom Miller, Stella Stephens, Cilla Bassett, Doreen Prosser, Betty Pritchard, -?-, Lillian Brazil. Front row: Phillip Bussey, Jimmy Sutherland, Christopher Nightingale, Joyce Cousins, Rex Bushell, Kay ?, -?-, the two Green sisters, -?-, -?-, Ian Smith, Doreen Smith. (Information and photograph by kind permission of Mrs Ilene Howard.)

Remembrance Cottage, Reading Street, once called Rosemary Cottage. On the night of 28 February 1917 a dud shell from a German destroyer struck this house killing the mother and one young girl outright and fatally injuring another. The family who lived in the cottage were named Morgan and the sons and father survived this catastrophe. The hole made by the shell was made into a window as a memorial to the departed and the house name changed to Remembrance Cottage.

Elmwood Farm House, 1906. In the 1700s Elmwood Farm was known as Josse Farm, after its owners the Josse family. The farmhouse is of the early Elizabethan era, its exact age uncertain. An interesting timber which came from the house and was used to repair a barn door bears the initials 'RS 1740'. The farmhouse consists of two buildings, the larger to the left is 200 years older than the smaller to the right, which is constructed of flint and chalk blocks, and like the rest of the house has no foundations. The resident owners are the Philpott family, farmers of long standing who in the past have farmed at Haine and Hopeville.

Callis Court, 1908. This magnificent building was the one-time home of Harry Hanoel Marks, a London financier who was chief proprietor of the *Financial News*, London's first financial daily newspaper, which he started in 1883. He directed its affairs until 1909, and was also MP for Thanet from 1904 until 1910 and a JP. Sadly Callis Court has been demolished and in its place stands the Royal British Legion Home.

Joss Bay, 1923. Named after the family of Josse, this quiet bay was renowned for its smuggling connections in the seventeenth and eighteenth century. In the distance the only visible housing is Kingsgate Castle. During the First World War, a large concrete dish approximately 15 ft in diameter was placed at the end of the beach facing out to sea. This dish picked up the sound of aircraft engines long before a human ear could, and so gave early warnings of approaching German aircraft or Zeppelins. This instrument was the forerunner of the radar system and was the first one ever used in the country.

Kingsgate Castle, 1910. One of Lord Holland's more spectacular follies, Kingsgate Castle has had many illustrious owners. Built originally as a stables and groom's accommodation for Holland House, the castle underwent extensive alterations in 1903 to make it look as it does in the above picture. The work was carried out by Paramours, the Margate builders, and the castle was then owned by Mr Jonas Levy. In later years Lord Avebury resided here, best known as the man who proposed the Bank Holiday, which we rather take for granted today. The castle is now private apartments and a restaurant.

The *Daily Mail* staff at Kingsgate outside the Captain Digby enjoying what is thought to be a 'waygoose', a term used by the printing trade for a 'knees-up'. The *Daily Mail* was Lord Northcliffe's own paper, so it is not surprising that the staff outing should travel to so quiet a spot.

The Captain Digby public house, Kingsgate owes its existence to Lord Holland who built it between 1763 and 1768. The Digby was once part of Bede House, half of which collapsed into the sea in 1809, leaving only the stabling which was built upon in 1816 and was used as a bibitory recess for men and horses (hostelry!). The Digby had a set of steps down to the shore which were obviously used by smugglers. It was here in 1857 that rescued men of the *Northern Bell* were brought when saved from a watery grave by the two Broadstairs lifeboats off Kingsgate Bay. Ironically, the Digby is named after Lord Holland's favourite nephew, who had a distinguished naval career catching smugglers.

The Kings Gate, Port Regis. Situated in the grounds of Port Regis, now a Roman Catholic school for delicate children, this gate once stood before Holland House in Kingsgate Bay in a fissure caused by an earth tremor on St Bartholemew's Day, so the gate was called 'St Bartholemew's Gate' until June 1683, when Charles II and his brother James, Duke of York, landed safely here after being caught in a squall while sailing to Dover. To commemorate their safe landfall, the king decreed the name be changed to Kingsgate. This gate was removed from its original position to the one depicted above in later years.

North Foreland and lighthouse. There has been a beacon or lighthouse at North Foreland since 1499. This aerial photograph, taken in 1920, shows very little housing development and how close the lighthouse is to the cliff edge. Guglielmo Marconi set up a wireless telegraphy station in a private house at Foreness Point, Kingsgate in 1899. In 1903 the GPO took over the station and installed it in a wooden hut alongside the lighthouse where it remained until 1923 when it was transferred to Rumfields. The present lighthouse dates from 1691 and has been altered from coal fired to oil; in 1930 it was converted to electricity.

Schools and Convalescent Homes

St Peter's Boys doing their physical jerks in the playground in 1909. All these boys would have known by heart the following ditty written about the school's headmaster Mr George (Skip) Taylor:

> Skip Taylor is a very nice man,
> He tries to teach us all he can,
> Reading, Writing and Arithmetic,
> And when he don't he gives us the stick.

St Peter's Boys' School (Mr Harry Dawes' class), 1914, with Skip Taylor, the headmaster. Built in 1838 as an infants' and girls' school, this school can trace its origins back to 1694 when Elizabeth Lovejoy of Callis Grange bequeathed £20 per annum for a teacher to instruct twenty poor children of the parish to read and write. The school was held in St Peter's Church but later removed to Ranelagh Tea Rooms on 6 June 1902 when the boys moved to the old school and the girls moved to a new school in Ranelagh Grove.

St Peter's Girls' School (Miss Strong's class), 1931/2. Back row, left to right: -?-, Marjorie Pentlow, -?-, Joyce Butler, Mary Beech, Olive Johncock, Betty Cook, Peggy James, -?-, -?-, Vera Twyman, Joan Moss. Middle row: Dorothy Beacham, -?-, Peggy Lucas, Gladys Rowlands, Ivy Parker, Phylis Hills, Violet Foreman, Doreen Thompson, -?-, Marjorie Davis, Jean Roberts, Peggy Pearce. Front row: Elsie Attwell, Lily Hollands, Alice Chamberlain, Molly Chapman, Lily Groombridge, Ruth Parker, Rosa Dengate, Lily King, Sylvia Frost, Olive Pearce. The headmistress was Miss Wyles and the names were given to me by Mrs Marjorie Lawrence (née Davis).

St Peter's Babies' (Infants') School. This photograph is believed to have been taken not long after the girls' school opened in 1902. The school was built by John T. May, local builders, at a cost of £3,000. The ground it stands on was donated by Mr A. Cobb of Margate (the old brewery family).

Hildersham House School, St Peter's Road. One of the first preparatory schools in the St Peter's/Broadstairs area, the school was the brain child of the Revd Harcourt Charles Vaux Snowden. It opened in September 1890 with twenty-five boys, two teachers and the Revd Snowden as headmaster. The school, situated almost opposite Green Lane, St Peter's Road, was named after a village near Cambridge and was built on land once used for village fairs and as allotments.

Hildersham House School, 1909. The masters depicted here are Mr Arthur Snowden, the Revd Harcourt Charles Vaux Snowden (founder of the school) and his wife, together with Mr Masters. Seated on the left is Mr Morseby. The school survived two world wars only to be sold in 1971 and pulled down for housing development. One old boy of the school worthy of mention was C.H. Frisbie who (in 1918) was awarded the Victoria Cross.

Selwyn House School, St Peter's Road. Originally named Claringbould House and built some time in the late 1700s, this building was bought by Arthur Glyn Price and his wife in 1906, specifically to start a preparatory school. Named after Selwyn College, Cambridge, this school flourished under Mr and Mrs John Green, son-in-law and daughter of the originator's. Mr Green retired in 1972 and on the 21 July 1977 Selwyn House was sold to Mr John Blackwell (of Cross and Blackwell) who later turned it into flats. Its playing fields were used for housing development.

St. Peter's Court, Thanet.

St Peter's Court, Sowell Street. Built for Mr A.J. Richardson in 1899 as a preparatory school, and run by the headmaster, the Revd Ridgeway, St Peter's Court had the distinction of having two sons of King George V as pupils. Prince George, Duke of Kent, and Prince Henry, Duke of Gloucester were attending the school on their parents' visit on 25 July 1913. In 1926 A.J. Richardson retired and the Revd Ridgeway ran the school until his death in 1958. The Revd Ridgeway's son, Charles, was headmaster for a short time after his father's death before being struck down by a serious illness. The school was amalgamated with Wellesley House in 1969 and this famous building was pulled down and, along with the grounds, sold for housing development.

Wellesley House School, Broadstairs. The last surviving preparatory school in the area, built in 1897/8 and formerly known as Conyngham House, it was originally under the administration of C.H. Rose, Esq. MA, and set in six acres of grounds. The principal was Mr C.R. Taylor MA of Keble College, Oxford. The school's fine traditions are carried on today and among those pupils to have attended the school in recent years are the present Duke of Gloucester and his younger brother in the early 1950s.

Brondesbury Ladies' School, Kingsgate. Built in 1913 as a ladies-only school and situated next to the golf course in Convent Road, this school is better known today as Kingsgate College. Prior to this it had been a YMCA college and before that Glyn House School for Young Ladies. Its future is, I understand, linked with the education of Japanese children.

Brondesbury School classroom. The school was for professional men's and gentlemen's daughters and offered examinations as an option. Note the young lady at the front in a reclining position and the open classroom windows and doors allowing sea breezes to waft in.

Lindenthorpe School. This school, with two acres of playing fields, once occupied the area where Lindenthorpe Road and Linden Avenue are now situated. Run by Mr and Mrs W. Oak-Rhind, the school's 1884 prospectus promised 'a thorough English education with Latin and French at 50–60 guineas a term'. Mr and Mrs Oak-Rhind were the parents of well-known Broadstairs and St Peter's councillor, Mr Edwin Scobie Oak-Rhind CBE.

Stone House, North Foreland. Built in 1764 by Sir Charles Raymond of the East India Company, the house (once the home of Archbishop Tait, Archbishop of Canterbury) was converted to a school by the Revd Stone who, in 1895, sold it to the Revd W.H. Churchill, who was succeeded by his son Arnold as owner. Surviving two world wars, the school finally closed on 17 October 1969. Thankfully a preservation order has been placed on this house which now contains private apartments, so saving it from the grasp of the housing developer!

St Peter's Orphanage. Once situated behind Stone House in Lanthorne Road, this orphanage came into being as a result of an outbreak of cholera in London in 1866 which left many orphans. Sixty orphans were housed here either from London or Canterbury Diocese and the orphanage was named after Mrs Tait, the archbishop's wife. Six acres of ground from Stone House were set aside for the orphanage and on 21 December 1869 Mrs Tait and her children laid the foundation stone. Mrs Tait had lost five daughters in six weeks to scarlet fever, a tragedy which must have influenced her and her husband's decision to build the home. Archbishop Tait had himself nearly died of scarlet fever as a boy.

Orphanage children at play. The children are playing where North Foreland Golf Course is situated today. In 1875 a convalescent home was built in the same grounds as the orphanage but sadly both were demolished in 1953.

Metropolitan Convalescent Home. The Met, as it was nicknamed, was one of many convalescent homes for children with pulmonary diseases such as tuberculosis. In the background can be seen the goal posts of Stone House School football pitches. The Met was pulled down in 1986 and has been replaced with buildings more suitable for handicapped children.

St Mary's Children's Home, North Foreland. Originally known as Thanet Place, this beautiful building was the home of Sir Edmund Vestey who, with his brother, was owner of the Blue Star Shipping and Union Cold Storage Company. The grounds the house was built on were previously the lower playing field of Stone House School which were sold to Sir Edmund in 1927. He had this Italian-style palace designed by the architect Mr Edgar Ranger of Broadstairs. The cost was £100,000 and it took two years to build. On 18 November 1953 Sir Edmund died and eventually, after being on the market for a number of years, the palace was sold to a Roman Catholic order who ran it as St Mary's Children's Home until recently. It is now a residential home and the seven acres of grounds have been built on.

Victoria Home, Broadstairs. Situated on the corner of the Eastern Esplanade and Park Road, this home was opened by Princess Louise, Marchioness of Loam in June 1892. Built by W.W. Martin, a local builder, to plans by Mr T. Hunt, a member of the hospital committee, the home is now Stonebay School for mentally handicapped children. What price the rocking-horse the young boy is riding?

St Mary's Convalescent Home, 1912. St Mary's was opened on Thursday, 26 July 1887 by their Royal Highnesses Princess Christian and Frederica of Hanover. The home was built by Yerburys of Kilburn and the architect was Frederick New of London. The home accommodated 300 children and was eventually pulled down in 1958. The barrow depicted in the foreground belonged to Thomas Page Swaine, the Broadstairs photographer, whose premises were at 41 High Street, Broadstairs. (Incidentally, he also took this photograph.)

Broadstairs Town and Dumpton

Broadstairs Pier and Bleak House, 1880s. Bleak House stands like a lonely sentinel watching over the quaint old pier, built in 1490, with its wooden breakwaters stretching out towards the sea. The pier was extensively damaged for the last time in 1897.

Broadstairs railway station gates. This was the view which greeted holidaymakers on arrival from London by rail in the early 1900s. Both the Railway Hotel and Railway Tavern, seen in the background, were built in response to the influx of holidaymakers which came with the advent of the railway in 1862/3. The Railway Hotel was built in 1864 and the Railway Tavern a year later. The estate agent's offices on the right and the station gates have long since disappeared.

Cottesmore, High Street, Broadstairs. In 1910 the address of this house was St Peter's Road. Before 1913, St Peter's Road ended at Pierremont Avenue. After 1913, Pierremont to the Broadway became the High Street, Broadstairs. This house is now Gordon's tobacconists and confectioners shop, but in 1910 it was divided into furnished apartments. It stands directly in front of Stanley Place.

Pierremont House and Gardens. Pierremont House, built in 1785 for Thomas Forsythe and known as Forsythe's Folly on account of its being built in such a remote place, has been the holiday home of Princess Victoria (later Queen Victoria), Edward Fletcher, J.B. Arnold and L.W. Posnet, the latter using it as a preparatory school called Pierremont College. In 1927 Broadstairs and St Peter's Urban District Council bought the property and it became council offices. It is now a Driving Test Centre. This photograph shows a captured German field Howitzer which was on permanent display until the Second World War.

Broadstairs High Street, 1930, showing how little has changed at this particular spot. The only physical changes are the tram rails and overhead cables, taken down in 1937, and the railings surmounting Pierremont Park wall, donated to the war effort in the Second World War.

Disaster in the High Street, Saturday, 10 June 1911. After demolishing a lamp-post, pillar box and brick wall, a runaway steam roller belonging to Messrs Finns and Co. of Canterbury comes to rest outside Houghtons, the photographers, on the corner of Belmont Road and the High Street. No personal injuries occurred as the accident took place at 6 a.m.; the driver, Mr Fekins, was unscathed.

Belmont Road. Before being made up as a road, this land was once part of the estate belonging to the Maisonette stretching from Broadstairs railway station to Albion Street and bordered by the houses of Alexander Road and the High Street. The first houses were built before 1849; by the 1920s the left hand side had been completed while the right hand side was open ground surrounding the Maisonette. This large house was once the residence of Daniel Mason, owner of the Cherry Blossom shoe-polish company. It was later turned into a boys' school called Ashton College. At a later date all the grounds were sold for development, only the land consisting of Broadstairs recreation ground, which was donated by Daniel Mason, after whom Mason's Rise is named, was left.

Homeland, Belmont Road, 1916. This large semi-detached house served as a holiday home for senior girls from London Sunday schools. The girls, who could be convalescing, spent up to two weeks soaking up the sun and the famous Broadstairs sea air.

The Pedle Memorial. This typical, gas-lit Edwardian sitting room full of lace chair-covers and ornaments, derives its name from Mrs Pedle who was the matron of this home and who died in 1904.

Broadstairs High Street, *c.* 1913. This quiet scene is a far cry from today's traffic-congested roads. The London County Bank depicted here was built in 1901 and replaced a row of small shops. Opposite, where the gas lamp stands, is Eveling's the well-known drapers. In the distance on the right is Redman's the tailors, probably the last obstacle to be pulled down to widen the High Street.

Broadstairs lifeboat, *Francis Forbes Barton*, 1905. A moment in time captured by Broadstairs photographer Thomas Swaine of Broadstairs High Street. Depicted at the corner of Crofts Place (named after Mr Croft, one-time owner of Dumpton House), the occasion is a parade to collect money for the local hospital. Behind the lifeboat is the banner of the Ancient Independent Order of Oddfellows, Perseverance Lodge, whose members are marching behind wearing their ceremonial collars, as are the two brothers in the foreground. The horses pulling the lifeboat belong to Whiting's of Albion Street; the second horse was led by Mr W.J. Fuller who lived at No. 10 Crofts Place. (Printed by kind permission of Mrs Fuller, daughter.)

Queen's Road from the High Street, Broadstairs, 1920. To the left is the Broadstairs Baptist church built in 1907/8. The foundation stones were laid on Thursday, 31 October 1907.

Pierremont Avenue from York Avenue, Broadstairs, c. 1920, showing a remarkable variety of architectural designs. The building of Pierremont Avenue commenced in 1898 when part of the Pierremont Hall Estate was sold for housing development. In the foreground are the tram lines that led into Oscar Road and eventually the seafront.

Queen's Road from Ramsgate Road, Broadstairs, early 1900s. Note the lack of houses and the number of trees still left from the Pierremont Estate. The tram in the distance is seen ascending Queen's Road after turning from York Avenue.

The Prince Albert in Broadstairs High Street, 1909. This public house is thought to date back to the early 1830s and consists of five bars with an alleyway separating its public bar from the wine office. The layout was, to say the least, unusual. The old pub was alleged to have had an underground tunnel to the main bay which was obviously used for smuggling. However, this and the old pub disappeared in 1910/11 when it was demolished in a road-widening scheme and new premises erected further back on the same site. The pub was a favourite haunt of the Bohemian Concert Party who appeared regularly at The Lawn (later to be renamed The Bohemian), an open space for concerts not fifty yards distant from this site.

Mr Barnaschina, the Boko poet of Broadstairs, depicted here interviewing President Kruger of the Boer Republic on this political postcard of 1910. Mr Barnaschina, landlord of the Prince Albert public house from 1897, was a native of New South Wales, Australia, who loved to quote poetry, one of his rhymes being:

My ales brewed in Gravesend,
  'tis clear as bell,
And if you drink it you'll always
  keep well;
Influenza of you will nere get a
  grip
If of my famous whiskey you oft'
  take a nip;
And slim men I warrant will
  soon all fill out
If they stick to my advertised
  best extra stout.

Ye Olde Crown Hotel,
High Street, :: :: BROADSTAIRS.

Proprietor - - A. E. SMITH.

The Most Comfortable Lounge
:: :: in Broadstairs. :: ::

WINES, SPIRITS & LIQUEURS AT POPULAR PRICES.

Ye Old Crown Hotel with its mock-Tudor façade was, in Dickens' time, known simply as The Crown Inn and is most likely to have played host to the writer on many occasions as he lodged at a small cottage not twenty yards away in 1837. The Crown's beer was from Russell's of Gravesend who also supplied the Prince Albert immediately opposite.

Serene Place is one of the oldest untouched parts of Broadstairs, consisting of Bradstowe House, Lancaster House, the Serene House and Castle House. Bradstowe House was once an office for a local newspaper. The Serene House was built in 1603 and must be one of the oldest buildings in Broadstairs.

The Royal Albion Hotel, Albion Street, 1920. This picture shows three distinctly different buildings which combine to make up the Albion Hotel. To the right is the oldest part, once the Phoenix Inn, built in 1760. The centre portion was built in 1805 and the two parts became known as the Albion Hotel. In Dickens' time it was known as 'Ballards Hotel' after its owner, a great friend of the novelist. The hotel is now owned by the Roger family, who are descended from Lewis Marchesi, master baker who settled in Broadstairs in 1884, well known in the early part of this century for his delicious cakes and bread. Lewis Marchesi was a founder member of the Round Table, originally set up in Norwich.

Albion Street in Edwardian days, 1907. Next to the Central Restaurant is Parsons Library Reading Room and Stamp Office, the four seats depicted outside placed there for patrons who wanted to read *The Times* newspaper. It was even possible to hire a pianoforte from the Parsons sisters. On the left in the foreground is the old Rose Inn, later demolished and rebuilt further back.

Peaceful Harbour Street in 1913, looking towards York Gate. On the left is Neptune's Hall public house, followed by May's, confectioners, and Manketelow's, also confectioners. On the corner of Union Court is Charles Wilkes, the watchmaker. The large house opposite is Flint House. To the right is Boucher's Library, and in the distance is the famous York Gate.

The York Gate, 1905. Built by George Culmer in 1540 and originally named Flint Gate, the gate was later renamed after the Grand Old Duke of York. Built to keep out raiding privateers it was extensively rebuilt in 1795 by Lord Henniker. Note the 'To be Sold' sign attached to York Gate House. The purchaser may well have been Sir Francis Laking, physician to King Edward VII.

The Garden on the Sands. These gardens once belonged to York Gate House, where in 1883 there was a school for young gentlemen. In later years it was brought by Sir Francis Laking upon whose death the grounds were used as tea gardens. In 1925 York Gate House and gardens were brought by Broadstairs and St Peter's Urban District Council and, in 1933, the pavilion was built on part of the grounds. The area then became known as The Pavilion and Garden on the Sands.

Voi House and Tartar Frigate. The public house takes its name from HMS *Tartar*, a naval ship built locally. It became the haunt of sailors, fishermen and smugglers in the 1860s and was run by a character called Ned Crouch who carried a 'preventative man's' bullet in his back. A glance to the left shows a clock on the roof of the toilets. This clock has a plinth on which are the following words: 'To the memory of J.G. Marsh, who in a brave endeavour to save the life of another, lost his own – September 21st, 1903'. The clock was erected by public subscription when Mr Marsh died attempting to save Mr Albert Jackson, who also died. Mr Marsh was a bathing machine proprietor in Viking Bay.

'Snap' Johnson, Town Crier. Born in 1832, Mr John Johnson was Broadstairs Town Crier for over forty years. Nicknamed 'Snap', this old man could be seen at the regular times of 10 a.m. and 3 p.m. on the pier, plying the age-old profession of crying, giving local news. Not born in Broadstairs, 'Snap' went to sea in 1847 but retired to Broadstairs in 1861. He was also a part-time lifeboatman making his last rescue on the Goodwin Sands at the ripe old age of seventy-six. The crier who replaced Mr Johnson was a Mr King.

A SCENE ON THE JETTY
'SNAP' JOHNSON , THE TOWN CRIER
GIVES US THE NEWS OF THE DAY

Bleak House from the Harbour, 1901. Low tide leaves the small wherries high and dry. On the left can be seen the cluster of old fishermen's wooden huts now replaced by a more permanent brick café and toilets. Behind is the old Tartar Frigate before it was extended into the house on its right. Next to this house is the tarred clapboard cottage called Admiralty House, built in 1815, which replaced a watchhouse and cottage.

Broadstairs Pier, 1919. Called a 'queer old wooden pier' by Dickens, it has been the focal point of Broadstairs since it was first built by George Culmer in 1490. Destroyed three times by storms, in 1763, 1767 and 1774, it still stands today encased in concrete. Twice the width it used to be, the car park to the seaward side has been added. The pier was run by the Pier and Harbour Commissions until 1914 when Broadstairs and St Peter's Urban District Council took over its welfare.

Lusitania life raft. Bought at a Red Cross sale in London by Daniel Mason, whose home was the Maisonette off Belmont Road, this life raft came from the ill-fated SS *Lusitania* torpedoed by a German submarine off the coast of Ireland on 7 May 1915. It was presented to Broadstairs anonymously on 7 January 1917 and remained on the pier for many years. Its whereabouts today are unknown to me.

Broadstairs lifeboat, *Francis Forbes Barton*. This was the last lifeboat to be stationed at Broadstairs, depicted here after a practice launch from the slipway. The first lifeboat of Broadstairs was the *Mary White*, built by T.J. White of Cowes and presented to the town in July 1850. This was followed by a second lifeboat called the *Culmer White*, again presented by the company. Both boats were privately run until 1868 when the Royal National Lifeboat Institution took command of the station. Later, two boats, the *Samuel Morrison Collins* and the *Christopher Waud Bradford*, were stationed at Broadstairs until 1897 when the *Francis Forbes Barton* came on-station. Sixty-two years of service came to an end in 1912, a total of 269 lives having been saved.

Broadstairs lifeboatmen outside the look-out house on the pier. These men risked their lives to save many a sailor from the Goodwin Sands. Their names are sadly unknown to me. (Printed by kind permission of Mr Strevens of Broadstairs.)

Broadstairs Pier, 1890 is shown here just as Dickens would have seen it. It looks very different from how we know it today.

Sailing barge, Broadstairs. This unique picture shows a Thames sailing barge being unloaded in the main bay. In the days before any good road system, these barges were the best means of transporting goods from the major manufacturing towns. The barges never left empty, returning, as often as not, with coal-tar taken from the Broadstairs gasworks or lime taken from the limekilns at Popular Road, St Peter's.

High tide on the main sands in early Edwardian times. No exposure of skin to the sun in those days. The young lady with her back to the camera does not realize her Victorian bloomers are caught by the photographer for posterity.

Sea, sand and seaweed. Even in the 1920s, seaweed can still be seen cluttering the foreshore. Note the ballista-type diving board used by the young boys in this picture. It almost looks as though you could have been hurled up over the prom rather than dive forward into the briny.

'Penny a Ride'. A tranquil scene on the sands of the main bay. These donkey owners were strictly controlled by Broadstairs Pier and Harbour Commissions who ensured that nobody ran any businesses without a licence duly applied for before the Easter holiday. This would include bathing machines, a row of which can be seen in the distance.

Rake's lorry in the main bay, 1947. The problem of rotting seaweed wasn't so bad when most local farmers removed and used seaweed as manure on their land. Many locals remember Rake's lorries staggering up under York Gate full of seaweed. Here, one of Rake's lorries, axle-deep in soft sand, is about to be pulled out by Mr Bert Wootton on the tractor from Elmwood Farm. (By kind pemission of Mrs B. Wootton.)

On Thursday, 8 September 1926 a flight of five Shorts Singapore flying-boats made a courtesy visit to Broadstairs. The planes, the two above seen in the main bay at Broadstairs, were stationed at Calshot and were due to visit Ramsgate and Margate. Built by Shorts of Rochester, the flight was led by Squadron Leader L.A. Durston.

An open-air Sunday School Union sands service by the aptly named Preacher's Knoll, 1905. Mr Newton Jones of the Sunday School Union was granted permission to hold services here providing no collection was made or sports indulged in. Music was provided by the portable harmonium on the extreme right. No competition from ghetto-blasters in 1905!

Under naval escort at Broadstairs, 1911. Jack Tar provides the escort for the young lady round the dangerous Beacon Rocks at Broadstairs. Britain's navy at this time was second to none in the world, and was hugely popular with the public, hence Jolly Jack appeared on many Edwardian and Victorian postcards. This Jack was a crewman of HMS *Drake*, a light cruiser of the Royal Navy.

Louisa Gap at Low Tide, *c.* 1910. Not as popular as the main bay, this bay was thought to be named after Louisa Crampton, daughter of Thomas Crampton, the famous engineer born in Broadstairs. There are not many bathing costumes seen here; Victorian attitudes still prevailed when this photograph was taken during the last year of Edward VII's reign.

Louisa Gap, Broadstairs, once called 'Goodson's Stairs' after the farmer who owned this part of the foreshore. The picture shows a concert party in boaters and blazers. They are Mr Austin's Imperial Concert Party (see p. 120). In 1882 a pier was envisaged here extending from the centre point of Louisa Bridge in a south-east direction for 1,200 ft. The steps from the sands to the cliff-top were built in 1905 by Mr George Miriams.

Dumpton Gap, 1900. Formerly called 'Dodemayton', this gap in the cliffs was used by farmers to gather seaweed as manure for their fields. With the advent of the telephone it was decided to lay a continental submarine cable from this point across the Channel.

The cable ship *Fencible*, seen in the background, laying a submarine cable across the Channel to Ostend in 1914.

The Cunmor Oak, Dumpton Park. Dumpton Park once consisted of 48 acres of woodland and belonged to Dumpton House, owned at one time by the Earl of Darnley. Later, Robert Crofts, a gentleman after whom Crofts Place in Broadstairs is named, was to be the resident. Depicted here as a camping site, the great oak has long since disappeared under bricks and mortar.

Dumpton Park Tea Gardens, 1926. This bungalow was demolished in 1991. Seen here in the 1920s, the Dumpton Park Tea Gardens grew with the number of visitors and holidaymakers which came in the early 1900s. The bungalow was situated behind the Brown Jug on the left of the Ramsgate road. In later years, Dumpton Park became Broadstairs Park and Cricket Ground, and the tea gardens reverted to a private residence.

The Brown Jug public house, 1900. Situated just inside the Broadstairs boundary, this flint-faced pub can trace its ancestry back to 1795 when, apparently, there was a building here named The Queen's Arms Tap. By 1814 its name had changed to the current one, and this alehouse was used to billet officers in Napoleon's time. In the 1900s the establishment became a regular stopping point for brakes and visitors to Dumpton Park.

The three-legged pig of the Brown Jug. Owned by Cobb and Co., the Margate brewers, the Brown Jug had an unusual attraction for its clientele in the early 1900s: this three-legged sow, depicted above with her litter. In 1905 the publican, James Saunders, asked for the removal of seven pigs from the Brown Jug stables to Newington Mill because of the smell which affected his trade.

Broadstairs from the west, 1890, before the advent of tourism, a sleepy backwater surrounded by fields. There is no clock tower visible on Preacher's Knoll and, in the distance, the lifeboat sits jauntily on the old pier. Boiling foam denotes the presence of the Beacon Rocks below Preacher's Knoll and one can imagine the roar of the sea and the cry of gulls are the only sounds breaking the wonderful silence.

Castlemere Hotel, Western Esplanade in the 1930s when Castlemere's address was Nos 13, 14, 15 and 16 Western Esplanade. The hotel was run by Miss Margaret Knight-Bruce and Miss J.E. Bennett. In 1937 the hotel boasted a masseuse and an electro-therapist, Miss Mabel Margaret Price MSR, CSMMG, ME, LET. With these credentials one's stay was bound to be a healthy one!

The Vale, one of Broadstairs' oldest roads. Once called 'The Bradstow Lynch', it was a track which led indirectly to the old farm at Upton. On the right, in the distance, can be seen a tall spire of the Congregational church which was completed in 1871 at a cost of £1,250.

Westcliffe Road, 1925. On the right are the large houses, which are still very much the same, and on the left there are iron railings which enclosed the meadow used for grazing the Yarrow Home's tuberculin-tested cows. The meadow is now covered by houses and the Yarrow Convalescent Home is now Broadstairs Technical College.

St Basil's, Westcliffe Road, 1907. This grand, detached boarding house was once No. 37 Westcliffe Road. It was recently demolished to make way for Seaview Court, a large block of retirement apartments.

Laying electric cable alongside the Grand Hotel. To the right is the Victoria Gardens, to the left is the Grand Hotel. Depicted straight ahead is Rivera Mansions and Granville Road. In May 1899 Thanet Electric Tramways and Lighting Company Ltd were granted permission to supply Broadstairs and Margate with electricity. This photograph, dated 1900, was taken by the BICC company who supplied the cables for this project. The man in charge was Mr Murphy who was also responsible for electrifying the tramways of Thanet.

Jubilee Clock Tower, 1900. Built in 1897 for Queen Victoria's Jubilee, the Jubilee Clock Tower was a gift to the town by Harry Hanol Marks who paid for the project out of his own pocket. In 1949 a solid copper Viking ship weather-vane was made for the clock tower by Mr C. Hodson of Reading Street Garage to commemorate the landing of the Viking ship *Hugin* at Broadstairs in that same year. In 1975 the tower was burnt down due to an electrical fault, but was rebuilt by apprentices of Thanet Technical College to commemorate Queen Elizabeth II's Silver Jubilee in 1977.

Victoria Gardens, 1903. Once grazing land for cattle, the Victoria Gardens were officially opened on Tuesday, 21 June 1892 by Princess Louise, Marchioness of Loam, daughter of Queen Victoria. The gardens were laid out by Messrs J. Cheal and Son who donated a small tree for the princess to plant to commemorate her visit and the occasion. After the princess left, a public dinner was held at the Grand Hotel at 7 p.m. After dark various houses and shops in Broadstairs were lit up with coloured gas lamps and gem candle lamps to celebrate the occasion.

Grand Hotel, Broadstairs, 1920. Built in 1882 for Mr John Butterfield, the Grand was a very select hotel. Dances held on Saturday evenings in the ballroom were by ticket only or personal invitation of the management. People were vetted at the door by the doorman. Among the well-known people who have stayed at the hotel in the past are Sir Anthony Eden and Stewart Granger, the film star. Now known as Grand Mansions and divided into apartments, the opulence of yesteryear is still apparent. The houses to the right are of Queen's Gardens built by local builder, John T. May.

Victoria Parade, c. 1912, showing the Assembly Rooms (later Andersons Café), Dickens' House, Horrell's the chemist, the Albion Hotel and Marchesi's restaurant. Note the fine Victorian wrought-iron balustrades on the first-floor balconies of most of the houses which have survived until today.

Chandos Place, Broadstairs, 1912, known today as Victoria Parade. A typical Edwardian street scene with barrows and horse-drawn carts either delivering or selling produce. To the right are two gas lamps, the only visible means of lighting this part of the Parade. Note the iron railings which have long since disappeared.

Dickens' House, Broadstairs, c. 1905. Dickens' House is now a museum devoted to the author's memory. The lady who lived in this house in Dickens' time was the basis for Betsy Trotwood in *David Copperfield*. The building to the right is Horrell's the chemists. Mr Alfred C. Horrell lived in Dickens' House until his death in 1921. A member of the Broadstairs and St Peter's Urban District Council, he was always eager to promote Broadstairs as a pleasure and health resort. The chemists shop depicted here later became Ward's gift shop. It is now Suzanne's gift shop.

Promenade and Sands, 1910. Edwardian ladies with large hats and long dresses take a stroll along the promenade while, on the sands, Mr Marsh's bathing machines line the edge of the water. His competition for customers came from Wilson's bathing tents, erected in front of Eagle House Gardens. The time must have been before 1 p.m. as no self-respecting person bathed after this hour, and certainly no licences were issued to Mr Marsh or Mr Wilson to trade after 1 p.m. by the Pier and Harbour Commissions.

Broadstairs Promenade in 1923 with deckchairs in abundance overlooking the sands. The ladies' hats have shrunk somewhat and some are even showing ankles beneath their dresses! Of note are the iron railings depicted in the right hand corner of the photograph – these surround the entrance to Waterloo Steps which at one time went down the cliff and came out on the sands where the children's play area is today.

Broadstairs Promenade disappears, 1928. On Friday, 12 May 1928, in the early hours of the morning, part of the cliff and esplanade overlooking the Garden on the Sands collapsed leaving the three houses in Cliffe Terrace in a perilous condition. Mr and Mrs Hall and family who lived in No. 1 Cliffe Terrace, took these photographs the following day. Happily, there were no fatalities, although a policeman had walked across this ground not many minutes prior to the landslide.

Bleak House, 1900. Built in 1801 for Captain Gooch, this is Bleak House as it appeared in Dickens' time. In 1901/2 it was extensively added to by its owner Mr Barry who became bankrupt over the cost of the alterations. In 1911 the house was auctioned but remained unsold and the mortgagees offered the house to Broadstairs and St Peter's UDC for £6,000. It was reported that if this offer was not taken up the ground would be used for building purposes. Fortunately this never came about and the premises were later bought by Mr A. Batchelor, a well-known financier, who in 1934 landed on the lawn of Bleak House in an auto-gyro. The house is now a museum of Dickens' life and Broadstairs history.

Dickens' Memorial, Bleak House, 1911. This memorial was placed on Bleak House in September 1905. The designer was Mr Raffles and the bronze bust of the great author was completed by the sculptor, Mr John Adams of Acton. The stonework was carried out by Elliott's, the stonemasons of St Peter's Park Road, Broadstairs.

A rather unusual view of Cosy Nook and Bleak House in 1920. Bleak House has been altered and bears no resemblance to the residence of Dickens' desire, while Cosy Nook was at this time a small tea room serving morning and afternoon cream teas.

Clevedon Home on the Eastern Esplanade viewed from Bleak House. In the foreground are the roofs of the coastguard cottages and on the skyline to the left is St Mary's Children's Home which, like Clevedon Home, has been demolished. Copperfield Court now stands where the Clevedon Home once stood.

Holy Trinity Church, 1905. Built on ground once belonging to Bleak House, Holy Trinity Church was dedicated by Archbishop Howley on 15 April 1830 and was originally called Bradstowe Chapel and dedicated to the Most Holy Trinity. In 1856 the district became a new parish and in 1862 a tower was added to the church along with a clock bought by Thomas Crampton of Broadstairs. In 1871 the rectory was built with an endowment of £62 p.a. In 1924/5 the church was enlarged and the tower removed leaving the church much as Dickens had first described it.

Nelson Place, Broadstairs, 1922, looking towards Crow Hill. To the left is The Nelson public house, partially hidden from view by the trees. Built as a private house in 1805, it was not converted to a public house until 1815. The row of houses on the left beyond the trees were used to house some of Nelson's naval officers during the Napoleonic wars, while the cottages, in the left foreground, are even older and are flint fishermen's cottages. Alfred Harmsworth, later Lord Northcliffe, and his wife stayed in one of these cottages in 1899.

Linden Avenue, off Crow Hill. This avenue was once part of playing fields that belonged to Lindenthorpe private school, hence the name Linden. Mr Frank Muir spent his early childhood days here in a bungalow called Adstone. He started his education at Stone House Preparatory School and finished at Chatham House along with his friend from nearby Kingsgate, the Rt. Hon. Sir Edward Heath.

Devonshire Terrace, 1930s. A cul-de-sac in the quiet corner of Broadstairs off Nelson Place. Mr West, a Whitstable photographer, took this photograph.

Ramsgate Road, Broadstairs, 1934. This was the view as you entered Broadstairs from Ramsgate. On the right is Granville Road and the big house on the corner is Tettenhall, a large boarding house once run by Mrs Kenrick-Smith. The shop on the corner of York Street and Queen's Road is Dawson's the newsagents, known in the past by locals as 'The Furness'.

Entertainers

Uncle Mack, *c.* 1876–1949. No publication on the history of Broadstairs in the last century could be written without mention of Uncle Mack, the famous minstrel entertainer. James Henry Summerson (Uncle Mack) was born in London in 1876 and embarked on a career as an entertainer at the age of seven. In 1895 he arrived in Broadstairs with Uncle Godfrey's Minstrel Troupe and played every season until 1900. The dawn of the new century saw the emergence of Uncle Mack and his Minstrels in Broadstairs. His popularity grew and in 1909 he received permission to erect a small stage by the main steps in the bay. In 1916 Uncle Mack volunteered for service in the army and, although forty years old, was accepted. In the same year he introduced two ladies into his Minstrels. After the First World War, he started a White Night every Thursday evening, the first being on 2 July 1925. During the Second World War he did not continue his performances on the sands but gave concerts in aid of war charities such as the National Savings. He returned to Broadstairs in 1947 amid cheering crowds and pouring rain!

Unfortunately the years of hard work entertaining visitors and local townsfolk had taken their toll, and in 1948 a small notice appeared in the local papers announcing that Uncle Mack would not be returning the following season. On 4 January 1949 Mrs Summerson died and the following month on 5 February 1949 Uncle Mack died of a heart attack, aged seventy-three.

The earliest photograph in my possession of Uncle Mack and his Minstrels on Broadstairs Sands. The board in front of the portable harmonium has the date 1902.

Edith Cormack and Vye Maylott, the two lady members of his troupe, on stage with the Minstrels, Broadstairs Sands, 1920.

Reg Wakefield's Broadstairs Minstrels. Reg and his troupe took on the mantle of Uncle Mack in 1949. The troupe consisted of: Bert Hollins, M. Taylor, T. Fannel, Reg himself, Johnny Harrup and Dorothy Taylor.

Gwen Lewis and Entertainers. The company appeared at the Garden on the Sands where the pavilion stands today. They also appeared at The Bohemia and on the stage with Uncle Mack on the sands.

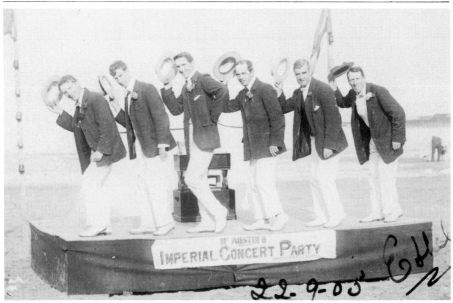

Mr Austin's Imperial Concert Party, 1905, at the sands of Louisa Bay. Their only form of musical instrument was a portable harmonium seen at the back of the stage. Two uprights supported small, candle-lit, coloured lamps used as lighting – costs were obviously kept to a minimum.

Norman Longford's Broadstairs Revellers, one of the larger concert parties from the 1930s with twelve performers on stage in 1936. Their venue was the Pavilion on the Sands.

The Bandstand, 1938, in its last location on Victoria Parade. Judging by the amount of empty deck-chairs, the weather obviously affected the size of audience for this outside venue. The band is unknown.

Palace Military Band, photographed by local photographer Thomas Page Swaine. In 1906 this band was conducted by Mr J. Wilson, Broadstairs bandmaster, who is seated in the centre of the picture and has a small drum at his feet.

Miss Dorothy Ward, schoolgirl. Young Dorothy in her school uniform of St Mildred's School, Broadstairs pictured outside her parents' shop, Ward's gift shop on Victoria Parade.

Miss Dorothy in her early twenties. She appeared in her teens in many of Thanet's leading concert parties. Her big break came while appearing at Ramsgate, when she was asked to perform in London Variety, and in the 1920s and '30s she was regarded as one of the best principal boys in pantomimes. Her career lasted right up until the 1960s.

Broadstairs Playhouse, Westcliffe Road, *c.* 1948. The building had been a cinema and then a repertory theatre which opened in 1927 under the management of Mr Robert Dennant. Sadly the playhouse was demolished in the 1980s.

James Grant Anderson, actor-manager of the Broadstairs Playhouse in 1927 who, with his sister Lena Anderson, also a talented actress, organized and appeared in many Playhouse productions. In addition Lena managed a repertory company in Ramsgate, alternating between Broadstairs one week and Ramsgate the next.

The entrance to The Bohemia, *c.* 1905. Through this ornamental gate came many patrons of seaside concert parties which appeared on the lawns belonging to this house situated half-way down Broadstairs High Street on the left hand side. In 1922 the Bohemia Concert Hall was built on this site.

Broadstairs Bohemians. This troupe of worthy entertainers started their career on the green adjacent to the Balmoral Hotel in 1895 but moved to The Lawn in Broadstairs High Street in 1905. Consequently, after considerable success, The Lawn was named after this concert party and became known as The Bohemia. Pictured above are Mr Tom Clare, Mr Robert Dennant and Mr James Avon. The ladies are sadly unknown to me.

The New Picture House. This cinema was originally called the Broadstairs Cinema and was built in 1912 for the Margate/Broadstairs and Ramsgate electric theatres. Its architect was Horace Dann. In later years it was renamed the Picture House and finally the New Picture House. Owned in the 1930s by Councillor Salt, the Picture House is the only cinema I know to have had a sliding roof and an arcade of shops leading to its front door. Sadly, on 17 February 1962 the doors closed for the last time, fifty years of cinema and Broadstairs history had come to an end. The last film shown was *20,000 Leagues under the Sea*. (Printed by permission of Mr Roy Henn.)

The Odeon, York Street. This cinema, designed by Mr P. Levitt and built in just nine weeks, was opened by Councillor B.J. Pearson and originally called The Royalty. The first films shown were *House of Rothschild* and *Krakotoa*. In the Second World War The Royalty was one of the first casualties of Hitler's bombing raids, damaged on 1 November 1940. It was re-opened on 3 August 1950 by Mr Jack Warner, whose *The Blue Lamp* was the first picture to be shown at the cinema on this occasion. In 1956 the Odeon was sold for redevelopment and subsequently demolished. (Printed by permission of Mr Roy Henn.)

Broadstairs Bandstand, 1904, situated here since its inception in 1893. In April 1905 the bandstand was removed from this site and placed on the Victoria Parade where it remained until 1952.

Pavilion and Garden on the Sands, around 1933. A rare shot of the stage erected within the Garden on the Sands, used by both Uncle Mack and Gwen Lewis.

Commerce and Traders

Reading Street Post Office, Grocery and Provisions Store, 1904, owned by Mr W.G. Johnson, known to all locals as 'Diddly' Johnson. In this shop most Reading Street people bought their daily requirements. Flanked by Welbeck Terrace on one side and Lawrence Terrace on the other, the shop is called The Village Stores today and is owned by another Mr Johnson.

Paramor Brick Fields. Mr Chapman and son with one of Paramor Brick Fields' horse and carts outside No. 3 Paramor Cottages. Behind Mr Chapman can be seen the wash-house belonging to No. 3. Paramor Brick Fields belonged to Paramor's, the Margate building firm, whose bricks were no doubt used in the construction of many houses in the area, including Kingsgate Castle.

Bing's Shoe Shop situated at the junction of Albion Road, Church Street and Beacon Road. The business was started in 1889 by Joseph Bing and originally traded in hand-made shoes, boots and repairs. During the First World War, Bing's was inundated with boots from the troops and local schools which surrounded the area. The business was handed down to two sons and a daughter but the shop now trades as a Chinese takeaway.

Thanet Useful Stores. In 1911 this general furnishing and ironmongers was situated on the corner of Upton Road and St Peter's Road and was owned by Mr Horatio G. Watson. Mr Watson and his family lived in the bungalow immediately behind this impressive shop. Sadly, there is nothing left today of this elegant emporium.

Kingsgate Post Office and General Store, No. 14 Percy Avenue, situated on the south side of the road. This sub-post office, like so many, doubled as a confectioners and general grocers store. Alongside was the Isle of Thanet Electric Supply Company Ltd sub-station.

G.A. Clarke Ltd Nurseries at No. 38 St Peter's Park, Broadstairs. The premises are depicted nearing completion in 1913. Clarke's were well known for their flowers and seeds, the business staying in the family until 1957, when it was pulled down to make way for a parade of shops and a block of flats (Willow Court).

Crouch and Son. These premises were situated at No. 17 The Broadway and remained a florists for only four years. Crouch and Son's Nursery was situated in St Peter's Park Road. As can be seen from the sign in the shop window, Crouch's dealt not only in flowers but also in canary guano, something unheard of today. The shop is now a confectioners and tobacconists.

H.E. Dixon's Garage at No. 166 High Street, Broadstairs in 1907. Dixon was sole agent for Clement Cars, manufactured in France. In later years the garage moved to Belvedere Road and became agents for Daimler, Chevrolet, Vulcan and Bean cars. The garage was also a member of the Automobile Club whose diamond-shaped sign can be seen above and to the left of the garage doors. This is the forerunner to the RAC.

The Tea Caddy, c. 1934. This was a restaurant on the corner of Vere Road and Broadstairs High Street. It started life as an office for the Broadstairs Pavilion Ltd in 1923. Later it was the premises of the Isle of Thanet Permanent Building Society until 1930 when it became a tea room. In 1936 it was taken over by Mr Paolo Mario Anselmi who ran it as a restaurant until 1938. After the war it remained a restaurant until 1956 when the premises became Beverley's Household Furnishers. Today it is an estate agents.

T. Fells and Son, a general grocers shop situated at No. 11 High Street, in 1912. We like to think that in the days of the glorious Empire, everything sold in our shops was home-grown or came from the Colonies, but the sign depicted in the bottom left hand corner of the picture clearly states 'Danish Butter', albeit at 1s. 1d. per pound. The shop now trades under the name 'Nick-Nacks'.

Staff at the Maypole International. In the days when service counted, staff at the International Stores located at No. 10 High Street, Broadstairs are seen here awaiting the discerning customers. From left to right: Mr Harry Brett, Mr Whale, Iris Scofham, Myrna Rook, Cilla Barrell.

Lawrence and Son's, grocers and wine merchants. Sited on the corner of Charlotte Street and John Street, around 1905, this family store also had premises in Ramsgate, and was established in 1881. The delivery van must have been one of the earliest to be seen in Broadstairs, and points to the fact that Lawrence and Son's must have been a thriving business in the early 1900s.

T. Maitland's, grocers. Mr and Mrs Thomas Jasper Maitland pose proudly for a photograph outside No. 4 York Street, Broadstairs, around 1913. By 1916 the shop had been taken over by R.G. Howard. When the photograph was taken Mr Howard lived next door (and also traded as a greengrocer). Over the years the shop has been many things, but at the time of writing it is a greengrocers.

W.P. Blackburn's Depository and Undertakers was in Buckingham Road, Broadstairs. There were no delivery vans when this photograph was taken, only horse-drawn carts and old-fashioned hand barrows. The Blackburn Depository was in later years taken over by Thompson's Removal Agents. The last Blackburn's initials were W.E., for William Edward Blackburn (WEB), so his staff called him 'Spider' behind his back.

Interior of Blackburn's shop at No. 5 York Street, Broadstairs. The queen post beams depicted in the roof are still an unusual feature of this shop today. The Blackburns were a well-known Broadstairs family who could trace their ancestors back to the sixteenth century. George Blackburn established the business in the 1840s and was a member of the Broadstairs and St Peter's Local Governing Board. Sadly the last member of the family died in 1952. The business is now a limited company.

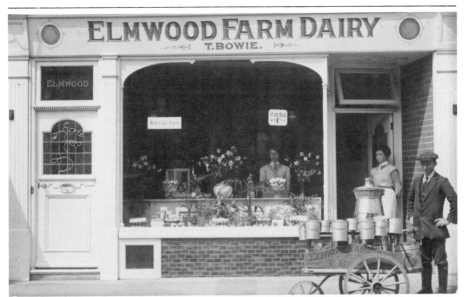

Elwood Farm Dairy shop, around 1913, was located at No. 24 York Street, Broadstairs, and was owned by Mr Tom Bowie. The hand delivery carts were nicknamed 'milk prams' because of their close resemblance to the baby prams of the era. The large churn held 16 gallons, and prior to the introduction of milk bottles, you had to have your own containers, i.e. milk jugs, for the milkman to dispense his wares. The containers surrounding the milk churn were his measures for this purpose.

Victoria Fish and Poultry Store was located at No. 21 Albion Street, Broadstairs in 1907, and was owned by Mr W.H. Carter from 1897 until 1911. The business was later purchased by Mr Frederick William Watling, another fishmonger. Mr Carter is on the extreme left. The shop today is the Myrofora restaurant.

Balmoral Hotel. Located in Albion Street facing the sea, and once owned by a Mr Richardson, one-time owner of Wrotham House, the Balmoral was originally an old coaching inn with a cobble-stone yard to the rear of the premises. The hotel also owned the small green situated on the opposite side of the road adjoining the promenade. Concert parties such as The Bohemians were employed here to entertain the patrons. The green is now owned by Thanet Council.

Mr John Stupples. In the early 1900s Mr Stupples could be seen at his Boot and Shoe Warehouse at No. 42 Albion Street. Born in 1835, he lived to the ripe old age of eighty-one, and his knowledge of local history was extensive. At the age of twenty-one he, along with others, helped to drag the two Broadstairs life-boats, the *Mary White* and *Culmer White*, over land to Kingsgate Bay, and there effected a daring rescue of twenty-three American sailors from the *Northern Bell*. During the rescue he nearly lost his life when gale-force winds threatened to blow him over the edge of the cliff.

The Two World Wars and the Fire Brigade

The Broadstairs and St Peter's Fire Brigades in competition with those from Deal and Sandwich at the home of Mr Edmund F. Davis of St Peter's Cottage, Sowell Street, St Peter's on 15 September 1879. The competition took place two years after the brigade was formed in 1877. The first captain of the brigade was Mr Henry E. Davis, brother of Edmund, and the competition was won by Deal, with Broadstairs second and Sandwich third.

Broadstairs and St Peter's Fire Brigade, 1900, outside the Broadway Fire Station. Note the horse-drawn 'Merryweather' engine. The firemen are, back row, left to right: G.B. Austen, G. Love, H. Turner, J. Temple, W. Nutting and W.C. Hills. Front row: F. Andrews, W. Pemble, Thomas Ferrier (superintendent), -?-, A. Brisley. (Photograph courtesy of Kent Fire Brigade Museum, Maidstone.)

Broadstairs and St Peter's Fire Brigade, 1921. Depicted here is the first motor appliance to be purchased by the Urban District Council. Back row, left to right: Arthur Bates, A. Smith, F. Burrows, W. Bayford, P. Moodie and F. Summers. Front row: W. May (turncock seconded from Water Department of Broadstairs and St Peter's UDC), G. Austen (superintendent), Captain Keith Jones (CO), L. Wilson, W. Jarman OBE, F. Day, W. Brown and William Heritage May. (Photograph courtesy of Kent Fire Brigade Museum, Maidstone.)

Edward Heritage May, 1921. Edward May was the first of two generations to join the Broadstairs Brigade. (Photograph courtesy of Mrs May.)

Leading Fireman Edward May. Ted May was the eldest son of Edward Heritage May. He served in the fire service for thirty-six years, finishing his time at Broadstairs station. He joined in 1927 and attended his first fire on 11 November 1927. (Photograph courtesy of Mrs May.)

Broadstairs fireman Kenneth May, of the Broadstairs Brigade, the second son in the May family to serve in the fire service, depicted here wearing the treasured brass helmet and full uniform. (Photograph courtesy of Mrs May.)

Fireman Walter Pemble outside No. 13 Grosvenor Road, Broadstairs, 1940. Sadly Walter Pemble was one of the five firemen to lose their lives in a bombing raid in Broadstairs on Saturday, 16 August 1941. The other firemen were: Arthur Bates (CO), W.D. Hammond, Sub-Officer P.C.R. Spice, and F. White. (Photograph courtesy of Mrs May.)

National Fire Service appliance, St Peter's, 1941. Broadstairs and St Peter's Fire Brigade were amalgamated into the Auxiliary Fire Service in 1938 but by 1941, because of the outbreak of the Second World War and the manpower shortage caused by the Blitz, they became part of the National Fire Service. The brigade is depicted here in a standard wartime Dennis appliance at St Peter's recreation ground. The fireman in the front seat is Leading Fireman Ted May. In 1945 the National Fire Service was disbanded and Broadstairs Fire Brigade came under the control of Kent County where it has remained ever since.

Fairfield House, once the home of Norman Craig, MP for Thanet from 1910 to 1919. In the First World War the house was used as a Voluntary Aid Detachment hospital, but in the Second World War it became the South East Kent Fire Brigade Headquarters. Setting up a 24-hour watch system, the brigade deployed many local men and women who spent countless hours in the cellars directing fire crews to the scenes of bombing devastation in south-east Kent.

The administrative staff of D Division National Fire Service at Fairfield House, Broadstairs in 1943. Back row, left to right: Joan Kilgannon, Pat Hill, Johnny Johnstone, Doreen Condon, Olive Brazil, Minnie Mirams and May Bennett. Middle row: Joan Milgate, Doreen Edwards, Helen Holness, Eva Deveson. Front row: Elsie Hammond, Pauline Ward, 'Kingie' King, Mickie Brown. They were hailed by the local press as the 'Ladies with Burning Ambition'. I am indebted to Mrs King for this photograph.

Blue Watch, Fairfield House, 1942. The following personnel are on an exercise. Left to right: Jean Pettit (now my stepmother), Edna Bracey (lying down), Molly Lucas and Hilda Cox on the stirrup pump.

Broadstairs Fire Station, 1968. Broadstairs' first fire station was next to the Dolphin public house in Albion Street, but by the 1880s it had been re-sited in St Peter's Park Road near the Broadway, Broadstairs. On Sunday, 3 August 1941 a stick of bombs was dropped on the Broadway damaging the fire station and injuring two firemen. The above station lasted until 1970. On Friday, 30 March 1973, a new Thanet Fire Station was opened at Westwood leaving Broadstairs without its own fire station.

Broadstairs mourns, 29 August 1941. The funeral procession of the five Broadstairs firemen killed in the air raid on Saturday, 16 August 1941 wends its way under the railway bridge past Cramptons Tower and the post office to St Peter's Church where all five were buried with due honours. (Courtesy of the *Isle of Thanet Gazette*.)

Councillors prepared, 1939. Councillors of Broadstairs and St Peter's Urban District Council try on their gas masks in the grounds of Pierremont House Park. Second and third from the front are B.J. Pearson and Councillor Minter, and bringing up the rear is Councillor Harry Noble (known as 'The Mayor of St Peter's').

Boer War, 1901. The armoured train depicted here was part of South Africa's Durban defences against the Boers. Standing on the ground third from the right is Mr Robert White of Osbourne Road, who was part of the Naval Brigade, but who in later life became woodwork and PT master at St Peter's Court Preparatory School, Sowell Street, St Peter's.

Kent cyclists' camp, 1914, sited in a large meadow behind Reading Street church. The meadow was part of Callis Court Farm, then owned by Harry Hanoel Marks, and the camp was struck before its two-week duration was completed as war was declared on 4 August 1914. One cannot help but wonder how many of these young men survived the next four years.

Guarding the Café, Harbour Street, 1915. Two stalwarts of the Empire mount guard outside the small café situated at the bottom of Harbour Street opposite to where the Mad Chef's Bistro is today. The men are believed to be from a Reserve Battalion.

Broadstairs Main Bay, July 1915, showing a squadron of mounted yeomanry. Depicted in the background is Eagle House and, to the right, York Gate House and Gardens. The sender of this postcard is Frederick Drake of Gillingham who is one of the men astride a horse. Evidently his squadron had just finished bathing horses in the sea. The postcard, posted in Canterbury, was sent to his mother, Mrs J.R. Drake, at No. 249 Napier Road, Gillingham, Kent.

Yarrow Military Hospital, 1916. The Yarrow Home served as a military hospital during the First World War and in 1916 was taken over by the Canadian Medical Services. All these men seen here are wearing the standard hospital uniform of light blue tunics and trousers with a white collar as issued by the British Army. No wonder they are smiling: their wounds are serious enough to warrant their being sent home, or, as they said in those far off days, 'they had copped a Blighty One'. After 1919 the Yarrow reverted back to its former role as a children's home.

Armistice Day, Kingsgate, 11 November 1918. The war to end all wars had come to an end, as is clearly seen in the expression on these mens' faces. The exact location is unknown.

Unveiling the War Memorial. In June 1923 a Guard of Honour from all three Armed Services, along with Public Services, surrounded the memorial to the men of St Peter's and Broadstairs who never came back. The site of the memorial was where a Gatekeeper's Lodge had stood beside the entrance to Pierremont Hall in Pierremont Avenue.

Sport Societies and Hobbies

Dinghy racing off Broadstairs, 1950. The Broadstairs Sailing Club was formed in May 1936 and its first commodore was Mr H.A. Dipple of Upton Road, St Peter's, ably assisted by the hon. secretary Mr D.R. Boult. The hard work of these two men and their successors has produced a very successful club.

The Sparks Football Club, 1901. This team was formed mainly from workers of the Isle of Thanet Tramways Company Depot, St Peter's, hence the name 'Sparks'. Back row, left to right: A.B. Impett, G. Merger, G. Welham, J. Lomax, D. Campbell, H. Burman (Captain), G. Warner, F. Hewitt (referee). Middle row: C. Willis, R. Stevens, W. Davis, A.A. Tyler, Esq. (President and Manager), G. Chapman, A. Cuthbert, R. MacKelvie. Front row: W. Keen, R. Johnson, A. Olive ('Sooty'), C. Hough, D. Tyler.

Thanet Electric Football Club, 1929/30. The players and officials had their photograph taken in a field at Callis Court. Back row, left to right: Colin Wardell, Harry Gilham, Abe Childs, Charlie Rogers, Bill Duff, Bob Kennet. Middle row: George Chapman, Jack Friar, -?-, Jack Fletcher, -?-, Sammy Smith, Charlie Parker. Front row: Bert Paramor, Ted Groome. (My grateful thanks to Mr George Everest for the names of these teams.)

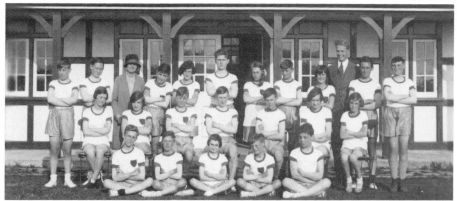

The Thanet Schools Sports Team, 1928, outside the pavilion in St Peter's recreation ground. The team were drawn from Thanet Schools and competed in the Kent Schools Sports at Maidstone on 23 June 1928. The team consisted of many Holy Trinity School athletes and was as follows. Back row: Stan Clark, William Hiller, Birchington School teacher, ? Bowles, Kathleen Terry, Ernest Derby, Birchington schoolgirl, ? Kemp, Mary Robinson, Mr Stolten (Holy Trinity Schoolmaster), Frank Croome, Birchington schoolboy. Middle row: Birchington schoolgirl, Eilene Pond, John Cock, Bill Wilson, Westgate schoolboy, ? Gifford, ? Peirce. Front row: Laurie Kitchen, ? Foad, Phyllis Shepherd, -?-, Ken McGavin.

Holy Trinity School Athletics Team, 1927. The pride of Dr Thomas Stud's Academy were as follows. Back row, left to right: Mr T.O. Stud, Mr S.W. Stolton (teacher and goalie for Broadstairs Football Club), Mr Yardsbury Bowden (Holy Trinity teacher). Back row: Bill Stannard, Jack Tolhurst, ? Maitland, Frank Croome, W. Gillet, Ken Ballard, ? Hiscock, Cyril Sheperd. Middle row: Ken McGavin, Len Wood, Ernie Derby, Bill Wilson, Norman Dixon, Bill Hiller, Stan Clark. Front row: -?-, Vic Hiller, Charlie Boulding, -?-, Stan Baxter.

Official opening of Broadstairs Bowling Green, 15 May 1909. The first game was played between bowlers from the Hero and Temple Bowling Clubs. The green was laid out under the direction of Mr Andrew Rae, the well-known expert. The green was situated behind the Eastern Esplanade and there were seven tennis courts included in this area. To the left of the bowling green is the Metropolitan Children's Home.

Opening of new bowling green, 1922. The occasion was the official opening of a new bowling green at the Memorial Recreation Ground, Mason's Rise. The cost of the green was £148 19s. 7d., £28 18s. 7d. in excess of the original estimates. Mr Ward, assistant town clerk, eyes up the jack and keeps a firm grip on his pipe, watched by Councillor Tommy Pemble in the bowler hat on the left. Next to him is Councillor Mr E.K. Minter.

North Foreland Golf Club was originally known as Kingsgate Golf Club and was formed in 1903. The ground was bought by Lord Northcliffe and laid out as a 13-hole course, the first 100 members were given free membership, and the secretary was L.H. Bacmeister. This postcard shows the first clubhouse, later known as 'The Nor-ard' or 'Norads' when converted back to a private house. The tall building behind and to the left of the clubhouse is Rose Tower, once situated just off the Convent Road. The course was enlarged to 18 holes in June 1913.

The Thatched House, 1930. Originally designed for Lord Northcliffe as an entry for the *Daily Mail*'s first Ideal Homes Exhibition in 1920, the Thatched House won first prize (hardly surprising as Lord Northcliffe owned the *Daily Mail*!!). It was dismantled at Olympia and re-erected on the golf course near Elmwood Road. One member of the golf club who will go down in history books is Miss Diane Fishwick who, in 1930, won the British Women's Open Golf Championships at Formby. Miss Fishwick lived in Reading Street as a child, not two minutes walk from the North Foreland Golf Club.

St Peter's Old Boys' Cricket Team, 1950s. Among the players depicted here are, back row, left to right: Arthur Dengate, Bert Brett, Harry Ford, Ted Harris, Ted Faulkener, John Epps, Ray Davis, Arthur Ovenden. Front row: Tommy Bing (one-time player for Tottenham Hotspur), Ron Davis, Bill Sampson, Bob Prett, Bomber Mills. At the front: Roy Farthing (mascot). This photograph was taken outside the pavilion, St Peter's recreation ground.

St Peter's Old Boys' first and reserve teams, 1957/8. Back row, left to right: Ted Harris (manager and coach), Pete Solly, Gordon Coker, John Epps, John Brenchley, Roy Rolands, Colin Hatchet, -?-, Jimmy Spain, Bob Prett, Arthur Ovenden, Alan Cowl, Tim Ward, Peter Delo. Front row: Dave Brazil, Roy Barber, Henry Bing, Tony Jefferies, Eric Horn, Bob Bugden, Colin Winterburn, Ginger Cousins, Dennis Wigginton, Norman Fashan, Terry Cooper. This season saw St Peter's Old Boys' first team win three major trophies in the Thanet Football League, a feat never to be repeated.

Left: The Rt. Hon. James Lowther, MP for Thanet, who in 1899 donated the Isle of Thanet Football League Cup pictured right. In 1906/7 the cup was won by Broadstairs Football Club.

Pigeon fanciers trophies, Broadstairs. A most unusual postcard depicting the prizes won by pigeons belonging to the Revd T.C. Wild of The Bays, North Foreland, Broadstairs. This house was situated next to St Georges' Private School on the Foreland. Mr Harry Newman, the manager depicted above, lived in St Margaret's, Beacon Road, St Peter's. The Reverend was obviously a successful racer of pigeons.

St Peter's Brownies, 1919, depicted here under the watchful eye of a Guide, believed to be Miss Hope Brandreth. Originally called the 'Rosebuds', Brownies are still in existence. Many private schools in the area, such as Haddon Dene School and Glynn House, had their own Brownie pack.

St Peter's Guides and Rosebuds, c. 1917. One of the earliest photographs of 1st St Peter's Guides which used to meet at Ranelagh Grove Assembly Rooms (once the old school-room). (My grateful thanks to Miss White of St Peter's for both these treasured photographs.)

St Peter's Cubs, 1924, brewing up at St Peter's Cubs Camp, Stanley Road, Broadstairs. The man on the right is Mr Hennessey, Cub and Scoutmaster, and the lady in the centre is Miss Bradfield (later Mrs Hennessey, the Akela). The man who started the St Peter's Wolfcubs in 1915 was the Revd E.W. Trevor MA, curate of St Peter's, who was sadly killed in France on 14 November 1916. Mr Hennessey was schoolmaster at St Peter's Boys' School and was the first Scoutmaster of 'Earl Haig's Own' Boy Scouts, as St Peter's troop was first known. (My grateful thanks to Miss White for this information.)

St Peter's Girls Brigade, c. 1924. This brigade still meet at the Baptist chapel in Vicarage Street, St Peter's. The occasion and location depicted above are unknown to me but the following were on photo-parade for the occasion. Front row, left to right: Captain Hilda Hooper, -?-, Grace Sylvester, Nora Stevens, Violet Brooks, Peggy Lucas, -?-, Mary Whittle, standard-bearer Dorothy Wood, Pam Farthing, -?-, Dorren Supples. Officer on the right at the back is Lt. Nellie White. (Many thanks to Mrs Reg Stockwell for the identification of the above.)

Compton, No. 37 Luton Avenue, Broadstairs, 1930. This imposing house was the home of Mr and Mrs Ernest Perry. Mr Perry was brother and partner in the family business of well-known coal merchants, J. Perry and Co. Ltd. Both he and his wife became Justices of the Peace and were keen social workers, founding the St Luke's Football Club in 1914 and acquiring the football ground at Dumpton for the sum of £2,000 in 1928. Sadly, Mr Perry died in 1931.

Mr and Mrs E. Perry, 1928, in the garden of Compton. Mrs Perry became the first chairwoman of Broadstairs Townswomen's Guild. The first meeting was held at her home in 1945. Mrs Perry died at York House Nursing Home, Broadstairs on 9 April 1970, at the grand old age of ninety-three, holding the position of president of the Townswomen's Guild.

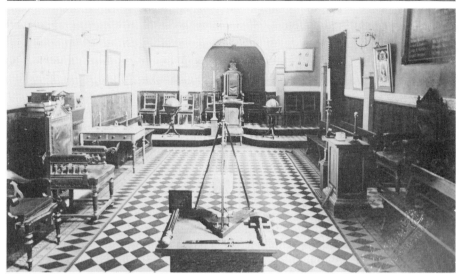

The interior of the Broadstairs Freemasons Hall laid out in ceremonial order in 1904. The official name of the lodge is Bradstowe Lodge, No. 2448. The photographer who took this picture was Mr Thomas Page Swaine of No. 41 High Street, Broadstairs, who was Worshipful Master of the Lodge in 1903.

Broadstairs Freemasons in their ceremonial regalia posing outside their hall in Alexandra Road. Among the eminent doctors depicted here, the fourth man from the right is easily recognized as Dr Hugh Raven, and the man immediately to his left is Mr Robert White, woodwork teacher of St Peter's Court School, Sowell Street.

Acknowledgements

My special thanks go to my good friend Mr John Williams of Margate Museum who has provided me with his valuable time and information. I am also indebted to all staff of the Broadstairs, Ramsgate and Margate libraries for their assistance, especially Mrs Pat Gardener, Miss Iris Huckstep and Penny Ward.

Thanks also to the many postcard dealers and friends who have helped me amass my collection over the past years, especially Messrs Clive Baker, Mike Sturge, Tony Hazard, Bernard Mundell and the many members of the Canterbury and East Kent Postcard Club who have kept a weather eye out for any Broadstairs cards.

The following people deserve my sincere thanks too, for the hours they have given up answering questions – I hope they consider the end product worth their time. I have certainly enjoyed their company and only wish I could have spent more time with each. Thank you all:

Miss White ● Mrs Sally Wood ● Mrs Bourke ● Mrs May ● Mrs Janet Dean
Mrs King ● Mrs Marjorie Lawrence ● Mrs Jean Brownings ● Mrs Shelley
Mrs Reg Stockwell ● Mr Dick Clements ● Mr George Everest ● Mr Bob Prett
Mr D.W.K. Jones ● Mr Colin Wilson MBE, BEM ● Mr G. Noble
Mr Snowden ● Mr Mike Prescott ● Mr Stan Clark ● the late Mr Len Bing
the late Mr Alf Bing ● Mr White of the Fire Brigade Museum, Maidstone
Mr Ken Goulding ● Mr Silsbury
the Revd Sage and his wife of St Andrew's, Reading Street
the editors of the *Thanet Times* and *Isle of Thanet Gazette* for their
kind permission to reproduce the photographs

I also wish to extend my thanks to (Aunty) Kath Moseling and Sue Willis who did some typing early on in the book's preparation, and to Dot Toft, the lady who gave up many hours to help me put the final manuscript together. Lastly many thanks go to my father and stepmother, aunts and uncles – I could not have written this book without their childhood memories of St Peter's and Reading Street nor without the forebearance of my wife, June, and son, Richard, in sharing the agonies and excitement of getting this book into print.